New Roads and Street Works Act 1991

SPECIFICATION FOR THE REINSTATEMENT OF OPENINGS IN HIGHWAYS

A Code of Practice

Approved by the Secretaries of State for Transport, Wales and Scotland under sections 71 and 130 of the Act

Y Swyddfa Gymreig
The Welsh Office

THE SCOTTISH OFFICE

London: The Stationery Office

Applications for reproduction should be made in writing to The Copyright Unit, Her Majesty's Stationery Office, St Clements House, 2-16 Colegate, Norwich NR3 1BQ.

First published 1992

Eighth impression 1999

ISBN 0 11 551143 1

Preface

Recognition of Equivalent Standards and Testing

The requirement for goods or materials to comply with certain specifications or to undergo specified tests shall be satisfied if such goods or materials comply with equivalent specifications of, or have undergone equivalent tests in, another member state of the European Community.

The basis on which specifications and tests shall be adjudged to be equivalent is set out in Clauses 104 and 105 of the Department of Transport's Specification for Highway Works, published in December 1991, of which relevant extracts are reproduced below.

Clause 104: Standards, Quality Assurance Schemes, Agrément Certificates and Other Approvals

Sub-Clause 2

"Except where the specified standard implements or is technically equivalent to a Harmonised European Standard or to a European Standard adopted for use within the European Communities after 31 December 1985, any requirement for goods or materials to comply with the specified standard shall be satisfied by compliance with:

    i) a relevant standard or code of practice of a national standards institution or equivalent body of any member state of the European Communities; or

    ii) a relevant international standard recognised in any member state of the European Communities; or

    iii) a relevant technical specification acknowledged for use as a standard by a public authority of any member state of the European Communities; or

    iv) traditional procedures of manufacture of any member state of the European Communities where these are the subject of a written technical description sufficiently detailed to permit assessment of the goods or materials for the use specified;

provided that the proposed standard, code of practice, technical specification or technical description provides in use levels of safety, suitability and fitness for purpose equivalent to those required by the specified standard in so far as they are not inconsistent with the 'Essential Requirements' of the Construction Products Directive (89/106/EEC). This sub-Clause applies also to works only in so far as the means of carrying out such works are indivisibly associated with the goods or materials for which an alternative standard, code of practice, technical specification or technical description is proposed."

Clause 105: Goods, Materials, Sampling and Testing Goods and Materials

Sub-Clause 4

"Where goods or materials are accepted on the basis of an equivalent standard, code of practice, technical specification, quality management scheme, product certification scheme or Agrément certificate as provided for in Clause 104, testing and sampling as specified in or applicable to such an equivalent standard, code of practice, technical specification, quality management scheme, product certification scheme or Agrément certificate is accepted..."

Sub-Clause 5

"Where testing is carried out in another member state of the European Communities such tests shall be undertaken by an appropriate organisation offering suitable and satisfactory evidence of technical and professional competence and independence."

Contents

Appendices

Notes for Guidance

Foreword

Under section 71 (in Scotland, section 130) of the New Roads and Street Works Act 1991, an undertaker executing street works* must, when reinstating a street*, comply with whatever specification may be prescribed for materials to be used and standards of workmanship to be observed. The undertaker must also ensure that the reinstatement conforms to prescribed performance standards, in the case of an interim reinstatement, until a permanent reinstatement is effected, and, in the case of a permanent reinstatement, for the prescribed period after the completion of the reinstatement.

This Code of Practice has been approved by the Secretaries of State for Transport, Wales and Scotland under their powers in the Act for the purposes of sections 71 and 130; it gives practical guidance about the reinstatement standards required. It should be noted that if an undertaker fails to comply with his duties under section 71 or 130 he commits an offence. Compliance with the Code will satisfy the undertaker's statutory obligations; failure in any respect to comply with it, whilst not of itself an offence, will be evidence of a breach of such obligation.

The Street Works (Reinstatement) Regulations 1992, SI 1992 No 1689, made under sections 71 and 104 of the Act, and the Road Works (Reinstatement) (Scotland) Regulations 1992, SI 1992 No 1674 (S.161), made under sections 130 and 163, set out the requirements on materials, workmanship and standard of reinstatement of street works*.

This Code of Practice was prepared by a working party of the Highway Authorities and Utilities Committee (HAUC), and was the subject of extensive consultation with interested organizations. The following were represented on the working party: the National Joint Utilities Group (NJUG) (comprising British Gas plc, British Telecommunications plc, Mercury Communications Ltd, and the water and electricity supply industries in England, Scotland and Wales); the local authority associations (comprising the Association of County Councils, the Association of District Councils, the Association of Metropolitan Authorities, and the Convention of Scottish Local Authorities); and the Department of Transport.

The Regulations and Code of Practice will come into operation on 1 January 1993.

Enquiries about the Regulations or this Code of Practice should in the first instance be addressed to the Department of Transport, NGAM2, Room 3.14, 2 Monck Street, London SW1P 2BQ. It should be understood that this in no way affects the right of any person to refer a dispute or difference to arbitration under the Code.

Department of Transport
The Scottish Office
Welsh Office

June 1992

* In Part IV of the Act (applying in Scotland), "road works" and "road" are, respectively, equivalent expressions to "street works" and "street", in use in Part III (applying in England and Wales).

Definitions

composite construction	:	a structure where the roadbase is composed of lean mix concrete or other cement bound granular material, normally with bituminous surfacing layers.
cycletrack	:	a way constituting or comprised in a highway, being a way over which the public have a right of way on pedal cycles only with or without a right of way on foot.
footpath	:	a way over which the public have a right of way on foot only, not being a footway.
footway	:	a way comprised in a highway which also comprises a carriageway, being a way over which the public have a right of way on foot only.
flexible construction	:	a structure where the roadbase is composed of either bituminous bound material or granular material, or a combination thereof.
geosynthetic materials	:	materials in the form of membranes, grids, meshes, strips, strands or rods.
interim reinstatement	:	the orderly placement and proper compaction of reinstatement layers to finished surface level, including some temporary materials.
immediate works	:	works comprising the orderly replacement of excavated material, reasonably compacted to finished surface level with a cold-lay surfacing.
intervention	:	restoration of a reinstatement which does not comply with the performance standards to a condition complying with those standards.
modular construction	:	a structure where the surface is composed of setts, concrete blocks, brick pavers or paving slabs etc. laid on appropriate sub-construction.
permanent reinstatement	:	the orderly placement and proper compaction of reinstatement layers up to and including the finished surface level.
rigid construction	:	a structure where the surface slab also performs the function of the roadbase; is of pavement quality concrete and may be reinforced. Under certain circumstances, as defined in Section S7, a rigid road that has been overlaid may be deemed to be a composite construction for the purpose of this Specification.
SHW	:	Specification for Highway Works, HMSO - 7th Edition.
TRRL	:	Transport and Road Research Laboratory: with effect from 1st April 1992, re-named as Transport Research Laboratory.
traffic sign	:	has the same meaning as in the Road Traffic Regulation Act 1984.
verge	:	means the part of the highway outside of the carriageway which may be slightly raised but it is exclusive of embankment or cutting slopes, and generally grassed.

SPECIFICATION

S1. Introduction

S1.1 General

S1.1.1 An Undertaker executing street works shall carry out the excavation and reinstatement in accordance with this specification. Where this specification allows alternatives, the Undertaker shall select one of the options allowed. Regardless of which alternative is selected, the Undertaker shall guarantee the performance of the reinstatement for the relevant guarantee period and to the relevant standards.

S1.1.2 The reinstatement shall be carried out to a method which incorporates the highest degree of immediate permanent reinstatement appropriate in the opinion of the Undertaker to the prevailing circumstances.

S1.1.3 If, at any time during the guarantee periods, the reinstatement fails the performance requirements of this specification, the Undertaker shall carry out remedial action to restore the reinstatement to the as-laid condition. An interim reinstatement shall normally be made permanent within six months.

S1.2 Guarantee Period

S1.2.1 The Undertaker shall ensure that the interim reinstatement conforms to the prescribed standards until the permanent reinstatement is completed, and that the permanent reinstatement conforms to the prescribed standard throughout the guarantee period. The permanent guarantee period shall begin on completion of the permanent reinstatement and run for 2 years, or for 3 years in the case of deep openings.

S1.2.2 A deep opening is one in which the depth of cover over the buried plant or equipment is greater than 1.5 metres. Trenches that fall intermittently below 1.5 metres for lengths of less than 5 metres are deemed not to be deep openings.

S1.3 Road Categories

S1.3.1 Roads are categorised by this specification into four types each with a limiting capacity expressed in millions of standard axles (m.s.a.) as shown in Table S1.1 :

Category	Traffic Capacity
Type 1	Roads carrying over 10 to 30 m.s.a.
Type 2	Roads carrying over 2.5 to 10 m.s.a.
Type 3	Roads carrying over 0.5 to 2.5 m.s.a.
Type 4	Roads carrying up to 0.5 m.s.a.

Table S1.1 Road Categories

Roads carrying in excess of 30 m.s.a. are not included in this specification. Reinstatement designs for such roads shall be agreed between the Undertaker and the Authority, on an individual basis.

S1.3.2 The m.s.a. categories and structural standards referred to in this specification are those to which roads would be designed, at the time of the reinstatement, if they were new roads intended to carry traffic for a 20 year period, to the critical condition defined in TRRL LR1132 or TRRL RR 87. Each Authority shall categorise its road network on this basis and the Undertaker shall use the most current information available from the Authority.

S1.3.3 Where an Authority does not classify its roads as required by the specification, the Undertaker shall determine the classification of all roads, as necessary, and provide a copy of its classification to all parties concerned.

S1.3.4 In any classification, a zero growth rate shall be assumed until such time as valid data becomes available to allow an accurate assessment, and only commercial vehicles in excess of 1.5 tonnes unladen weight are to be considered.

S1.4 Footway and Footpath Categories

Footways and footpaths are categorised by this specification as follows:

S1.4.1 High duty - those designated as principal routes and used by an exceptionally large number of pedestrians.

S1.4.2 High amenity - those that are essentially of a highly decorative nature, and have been constructed and maintained to a high standard. Such footways & footpaths will usually be situated in conservation areas, holiday, leisure or ornamental centres, pedestrian precincts or where an Authority has maintained a policy of high quality paving in certain residential or commercial neighbourhoods.

S1.4.3 Other - those that are neither high duty nor high amenity.

S1.5 Alternative Options

An Undertaker may adopt an alternative specification for materials, layer thicknesses and compaction methods to take advantage of new or local materials and/or new compaction equipment, subject to the prior agreement of the Authority. There shall be no departure from the performance requirements during the guarantee period.

S1.6 Immediate Works

S1.6.1 There are circumstances when it is necessary to immediately reinstate an excavation, regardless of material availability etc., purely to enable traffic or pedestrian movement to occur on a traffic sensitive route. In such circumstances reinstatements may be completed using excavated material, properly compacted in 100 mm layers to within 40 mm of the finished surface level, and a minimum surfacing of 40 mm of bituminous material.

S1.6.2 All materials so placed which do not comply with the requirements of this specification shall be re-excavated and reinstated, to the appropriate interim or permanent standard as specified, as soon as is practicable but within 10 working days following the completion of the immediate works.

S1.7 Services within the Road Structure

Undertakers' apparatus shall not be permitted within the wearing course, basecourse or within 20 mm of the roadbase/basecourse interface in a flexible road, or within the overlay, concrete road slab or within 20 mm of the underside of the concrete road slab in a rigid road. This provision applies only to apparatus of 20 mm external diameter or less. Where other existing services or surrounds occur within the road structure, the method of reinstatement shall be determined by mutual agreement. All other apparatus greater than 20 mm external diameter will not normally be permitted within the road structure.

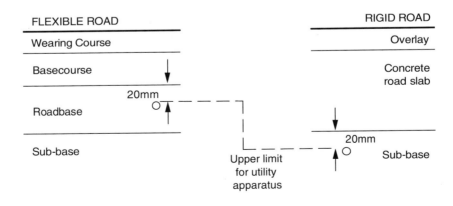

Figure S1.1 - Apparatus within the Road Structure

S1.8 Geosynthetic Materials

Where a road, footway, footpath, cycletrack or verge contains any geosynthetic materials, the Authority shall notify the Undertaker accordingly prior to the commencement of works, whereupon the method of reinstatement shall be determined by mutual agreement. In the absence of any prior notification, the Undertaker shall not be responsible or liable for the repair of any damage resulting from interference with any geosynthetic materials. If, in the absence of notification, any geosynthetic materials are noticed during the course of works, the Undertaker shall immediately notify the Authority accordingly. The Undertaker should make reasonable efforts to comply with any advice obtained from the Authority thereafter.

S1.9 Arbitration

Any dispute between the undertaker and the authority as to any matter arising under this Code shall be settled by arbitration as if it were a matter which under the Act is to be settled by arbitration.

S2. Performance Requirements

S2.1 General

S2.1.1 The following requirements shall apply to the immediate, interim and permanent reinstatements of all Undertakers' excavations. If, at any time during the immediate, interim or permanent guarantee periods the surface profile of a reinstatement exceeds any of the intervention limits, remedial action shall be carried out in order to return the surface profile of the reinstatement to the as-laid condition described in Section S2.2.1. No new guarantee period shall be required unless the cumulative settlement intervention limit is exceeded and any re-excavation and subsequent reinstatement agreed, as a result of the engineering investigation, has been completed in accordance with Section S2.5.

S2.1.2 For modular paved surface, the effective width of a reinstatement (W) is deemed to be the distance between the outer extremities of any modules that overlap the edges of the excavation; see Figure S2.1.

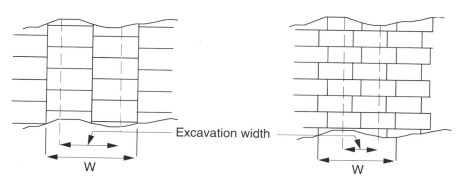

Figure S2.1 - Effective Width of Reinstatement - Modular Surfaces

S2.2 Surface profile

S2.2.1 As-laid Profile
The reinstatement of any surface shall be completed so that the edges of the reinstatement are flush with the adjacent surfaces and the reinstatement shall not show any significant depression in between. The maximum allowable tolerance at the edge of the reinstatement between the levels of the reinstatement and the adjacent surface shall not exceed ±6 mm.

S2.2.2 Edge Depression - Intervention
An edge depression is an essentially vertical step or trip at the interface of the reinstatement and the existing surface. Intervention is required where the depth of any edge depression exceeds 10 mm, over a continuous length of more that 100 mm. See Figure S2.2.

Figure S2.2 - Edge Depression Limits

S2.2.3 Surface Depression - Intervention
A surface depression is a depressed area within the reinstatement having generally smooth edges and gently sloping sides forming a shallow dish; see Figure S2.3. Intervention is required where the depth of any area of surface depression spanning more than 100 mm in any plan dimension exceeds the limits shown in Table S2.1

Figure S2.3 - Surface Depression Limits

Reinstatement Width W (mm)	Intervention Limit X (mm)
up to 400	10
over 400 to 500	12
over 500 to 600	14
over 600 to 700	17
over 700 to 800	19
over 800 to 900	22
over 900	25

Table S2.1 - Intervention Limits - Surface Depression

Earlier intervention will be required if the depression alone results in standing water wider than 500 mm or exceeding one square metre in area, at 2 hours after the cessation of rainfall.

S2.2.4   Surface Crowning - Intervention

Surface crowning is an upstand of the reinstatement above the mean level of the existing adjacent surfaces. See Figure S2.4. Intervention is required where the height of any area of surface crowning spanning more that 100 mm in any plan dimension exceeds the limits shown in Table S2.2.

Figure S2.4 - Surface Crowning Limits

Reinstatement Width W (mm)	Intervention Limit Z (mm)
up to 400	10
over 400 to 500	12
over 500 to 600	14
over 600 to 700	17
over 700 to 800	19
over 800 to 900	22
over 900	25

Table S2.2 - Intervention Limits - Surface Crowning

Earlier intervention will be required if crowning alone results in standing water wider than 500 mm or exceeding one square metre in area, at 2 hours after the cessation of rainfall.

S2.2.5   Combined Defect - Intervention

The intervention limits shown in Tables S2.1 and S2.2 shall be reduced by 20%, subject to a minimum of 10 mm, where edge depression and/or surface depression and/or surface crowning overlap.

S2.2.6   Handover Condition
At handover, at the end of the guarantee period, the surface profile of the reinstatement shall not be required to be superior, in any respect, to either the condition existing prior to excavation or to the condition of the adjacent surfaces at handover.

If, at the time of handover, the profile of the existing surfaces adjacent to the reinstatement is uniform and substantially superior to the surface of the reinstatement, the Undertaker shall carry out remedial work to restore the surface profile of the reinstatement to a condition consistent with the adjacent surfaces.

S2.3 Fixed Features

S2.3.1   As-laid Profile
All fixed features, e.g. kerbstones and related precast concrete products, channel blocks and drainage fixtures, surface boxes and ironware, shall be laid to coincide with the mean level of the immediately adjacent surfaces. The maximum allowable tolerance between the levels of the feature and the immediately adjacent surfaces shall not exceed ±6mm.

S2.3.2   Intervention
Intervention is required where the mean level of kerbstones, related precast concrete products, surface boxes and ironware does not coincide with the mean level of the immediately adjacent surfaces within a tolerance of ±10 mm. In the case of drainage fixtures intervention is required where the mean level does not coincide with the mean level of the immediately adjacent surfaces within a tolerance of +6mm to -15mm.

S2.4 Surface Regularity

S2.4.1   The longitudinal regularity of the surfaces of road trench reinstatements shall be monitored and compared with similar measurements taken along the adjacent road surface. Surface irregularities may be measured using the TRRL rolling straightedge.

S2.4.2   The number of surface irregularities recorded along the surface of permanent reinstatements, and iterim reinstatements where the speed limit is over 65kph (40mph), should not exceed the lower limit shown in Table S2.3. However, where the number of irregularities recorded along the adjacent road exceeds the lower limit, the number of irregularities recorded along the reinstatement shall not exceed the product of the number measured along the adjacent road and the multiplier shown in Table S2.3. Where the number of irregularities recorded along the adjacent road exceeds the upper limit shown in Table S2.3, or where the line of the road and/or the trench follow a level radius of less than 500 metres, or where the line of the trench is transverse or otherwise oblique to the line of the road and/or the traffic flow, or where the line of the trench is parallel to the line of the road and/or the traffic flow for less than 30 metres length, then the rolling straightedge shall not be used to determine surface regularity. In such cases, the surface regularity shall be assessed on some mutually agreed basis.

Surface irregularities not less than	Lower limit	Multiplier	Upper limit
4 mm	11	1.2	22
7 mm	2	1.2	4

Table S2.3 - Surface Regularity

S2.4.3   The upper and lower limit values shown in Table S2.3 are relative to a 30 metre reference length. For lengths in excess of 30 metres the limits should be calculated pro rata and rounded up to the nearest whole number.

S2.5 Structural Integrity

The requirements for structural integrity are applicable to both paved and unpaved surfaces.

S2.5.1 Cumulative Settlement

The cumulative settlement of any reinstatement is deemed to be the vertical distance from the level of the adjacent surfaces to the original surface of the reinstatement. This will include the thickness of any additional materials added during preceding remedial work. If the cumulative settlement of a reinstatement exceeds the limits shown in Table S2.4 at any time within the guarantee period, an agreed engineering investigation shall be carried out, jointly with the Authority, to establish whether or not settlement is likely to continue and to determine the extent of remedial action required. See Figure S2.5.

No new guarantee period shall be required until the re-excavation and subsequent reinstatement has been completed. Where it is necessary to re-excavate a reinstatement to carry out an engineering investigation, the subsequent reinstatement shall be deemed to be new and the guarantee period shall begin again.

Reinstatement width	Intervention limit Q			
	Normal ground conditions		Bad ground conditions	
Up to 1000 mm	1.5% U or 30 mm	} whichever is greater	2.5% U or 30 mm	} whichever is greater
Over 1000 mm	1.5% U or 35 mm	} whichever is greater	2.5% U or 35 mm	} whichever is greater

Table S2.4 - Structural Integrity

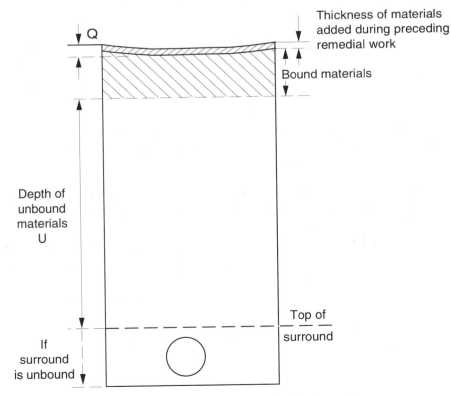

Figure S2.5 - Cumulative Settlement

S2.5.2 Bad Ground

Bad ground is deemed to be natural or made-up ground, between the bed of the excavation and the basecourse level, that contains any of the following :

a) materials that are loose or friable in their natural state and are incapable of providing self support at an exposed face;
b) Class E unacceptable material as specified in Appendix A1.
c) materials that are saturated, regardless of whether free or running water is present;
d) an excessive degree of rocks or boulders, loose random rubble, penning, setts or cobbles etc, at any depth where their removal during excavation could cause loosening of the ground adjacent to the excavation.

S2.6 Skid Resistance

S2.6.1 General

The following texture depth and Polished Stone Value (PSV) requirements are applicable to the surfaces of all interim and permanent reinstatements within any road category. There is no requirement to provide a PSV or texture depth that is superior to that existing at the running surfaces adjacent to the reinstatement.

Where chippings are to be embedded into a road surface, they shall be spread so as to give a chipping density reasonably matching that of the existing surface.

S2.6.2   Bituminous Road Surfaces - Texture Depth

1)   The texture depth of bituminous roads shall be measured using the sand patch method in accordance with BS.598 : Part 105. The minimum texture depth required at any site is shown in Table S2.5.

Location	Texture depth (mm)	
	HRA and surface dressing	Other surfaces
Trunk roads where the speed limit is over 90 k.p.h. (55 m.p.h.)	1.5 average 1.2 minimum	0.6 minimum
All other roads	1.0 minimum	0.6 minimum

Table S2.5 - Bituminous Roads - Texture Depth (Sand patch method)

2)   The entire reinstatement shall be divided into notional units of 18 m² maximum area and a minimum of 3 measurements taken on each area unit. Where more than 3 measurements are taken, the average texture depth shall be calculated for each unit from all results obtained.

3)   The sand patch method requires a minimum patch diameter, depending on the texture depth to be measured, and may not be suitable for narrow trench reinstatements. The appropriate minimum patch diameters required for the current BS.598 : Part 105 Sand Patch Method, are shown in Table S2.6. Subject to prior mutual agreement, a modified version of the sand patch test, using a smaller volume of sand, may

Texture depth (mm)	Minimum sand patch diameter (mm)
1.5	210
1.2	230
1.0	250
0.6	325

Table S2.6 - Sand Patch Method - Minimum Patch Diameter

be used on reinstatements narrower than those shown in Table S2.6.

4) If the TRRL Mini Texture Meter is to be used by mutual agreement, the method shall be in accordance with prevailing Government requirements.

S2.6.3 Concrete Road Surfaces - Texture Depth
The texture depth of concrete roads shall not be less than 0.65 mm, when measured by the sand patch method, or that existing at the adjacent surfaces, whichever is less. Where the existing road surface has been randomly grooved and the trench is less than one metre width, a brushed surface finish shall be allowed.

S2.6.4 Bituminous Road Surfaces - Polished Stone Value (PSV)
1) The PSV shall be measured in accordance with BS.812; Part 114. For the purpose of determining the required PSV reinstatements are classified into three categories according to the estimated degree of risk associated with the location as follows :

i) A - Potentially High Risk
Roundabouts, traffic lights, pedestrian crossing and railway level crossings; all including the final 50 metres of approach road.

ii) B - Apparent Average Risk
Major road junctions including the final 50 metres of approach road, steep gradients (over 5%) and tight bends (radius less than 150 metres at more than 65 k.p.h. (40 m.p.h.).

iii) C - Apparent Low Risk
Generally straight sections of road including minor junctions, shallow gradients and open or slow speed bends.

2) The minimum PSV required at any site is shown in Table S2.7.

3) Where an interim wearing course reinstatement is carried out using an aggregate that may not provide

Road type	Minimum PSV		
	A	B	C
1	70	68	57
2	68	63	53
3	65	60	50
4	63	55	45

Table S2.7 - Bituminous Roads - Polished Stone Value

the minimum required PSV, an additional surface dressing or slurry sealing treatment may be required. In such cases the PSV requirements shown in Table S2.7 are applicable only to the aggregate contained within the surface treatment and not to the underlying aggregate within the interim wearing course.

S3. Excavation

S3.1 Breaking the Surface

S3.1.1   Bituminous and concrete surfaced roads and footways shall be cut to the full depth of the surfacing at the initial stage. All loose materials shall be removed to ensure that the trench edge is in a safe and stable condition.

S3.1.2   When excavating in modular construction, the existing modules shall be lifted carefully, and stored for re-use.

S3.2 Trench Width

The trench width shall be such that adequate access is available for compaction of the surround to apparatus.

S3.3 Excavation

S3.3.1   All excavations in the road shall be carried out in a manner which avoids undue damage to the road structure. All excavating equipment shall be capable of carrying out the excavation to the required depth in any material likely to be encountered. Where practicable, damage to tree roots shall be avoided.

S3.3.2   The trench walls shall be even and vertical with no significant undercutting of the running surface. If undercutting occurs, measures shall be taken to fill any voids as soon as practicable or immediately after trench support has been provided.

S3.3.3   Excavations shall be protected as far as is reasonably practical from the ingress of water, and water running into them shall be drained or pumped to an approved disposal point. Any drainage sumps shall be sited so as to prevent damage to the excavation.

S3.4 Excavated Material

S3.4.1   All excavated materials that are to be re-used should be protected from excessive drying or wetting during storage. Additionally, these materials should be excavated, stored, handled and laid so as to avoid contamination and loss of fines.

S3.4.2   Excavated material unsuitable for re-use shall be removed from site as soon as practicable. Excavated material, if retained on site adjacent to the trench, shall be stockpiled at a safe distance from the trench edge.

S3.5 Side Support

The sides of all excavations in soft or loose ground shall, ordinarily, be provided with a side support system. The support system shall be properly designed and installed to restrain lateral movement of the side walls, and should be installed without delay. Supports shall be progressively withdrawn as backfilling and compaction progresses, and all voids carefully filled.

S3.6 Drainage

Any drainage disturbed during excavation shall be immediately notified to the owners, and restored to the requirements of the owner; see Section S11.4.

S4. Surround to Apparatus

Material details and laying procedures for the surround to apparatus shall be the responsibility of the relevant Undertaker, subject to the following overall requirements:

i) Class E unacceptable materials as shown in Appendix A1 and materials that contain particles greater than 37.5 mm nominal size shall not be used as surround to the apparatus.

ii) Preformed modules or other protective measures may be placed within the finefill or backfill, according to Undertakers' requirements.

iii) Finefill materials may be laid to a maximum of 250 mm above the crown of the Undertakers' apparatus and shall be adequately compacted, according to Undertakers' requirements.

iv) A foamed concrete mixture may be used for the entire finefill layer, or any part thereof, in accordance with Appendix A9.

S5. Backfill

S5.1 Backfill Material Classification

Backfill materials, whether imported to site or derived on-site from excavated materials, are classified as follows, and shall be used in accordance with Appendix A1.

1)   Class A - Graded Granular Materials
Graded granular materials with a maximum of 10% by weight passing a 63 micron BS sieve and with all materials passing a 425 micron BS sieve showing a plasticity index of 6 or less, determined in accordance with BS1377 : Part 2, Method 5.4, are classified as Class A graded granular materials and shall be compacted in accordance with Appendix A8. This class of materials shall include granular sub-base material Type 1 and granular sub-base material Type 2 (excluding natural sands and gravels).

2)   Class B - Granular Materials
Granular materials with a maximum of 10% by weight passing a 63 micron BS sieve are classified as Class B granular materials and shall be compacted in accordance with Appendix A8.

3)   Class C - Cohesive/Granular Materials
Mixtures of granular, silt and clay materials with between 10% and 80% by weight passing a 63 micron BS sieve are classified as Class C cohesive/granular materials and shall be compacted in accordance with Appendix A8.

4)   Class D - Cohesive Materials
Clay, silt or mixtures of clay and silt with at least 80% by weight passing a 63 micron BS sieve are classified as Class D cohesive materials and shall be compacted in accordance with Appendix A8.

5)   Class E - Unacceptable Materials
Materials listed as unacceptable in paragraphs 2(ii) and 3 of SHW Clause 601, shall not be used at any level, within the permanent structure of any reinstatement. Materials classified as unacceptable are shown in Appendix A1.

S5.2 Foamed Concrete

A foamed concrete mixture may be used for the entire backfill layer, or any part thereof, in accordance with Appendix A9.

S5.3 Chalk

Chalk may be used as backfill only after determination of its saturation moisture content and subsequent agreement on appropriate compaction requirements and backfill category.

S5.4 Additional Requirements

1)   Frost Heave Susceptibility
Frost susceptible material, i.e. material with a mean heave greater than 15 mm when tested in accordance with BS 812, part 124 (as amended by SHW Cl.705), shall not be used within 450 mm of the road surface; 300 mm of wholly bituminous material is considered to offer equivalent insulation and may be used as an alternative. Where frost susceptible materials already exist within 450 mm of the surface, such materials may be reinstated to the same levels. Similarly, where the existing depth of non-frost susceptible materials is greater than 450 mm below the road surface and the Authority requires such a thickness of non-frost susceptible material to be maintained, then, provided that the Authority notifies the Undertaker accordingly, only non-frost susceptible materials shall be used for the relevant depth.

2)   Maximum Particle Size
All granular backfill materials shall pass through a 75 mm BS sieve. All granular backfill materials used in the reinstatement of trenches less than 150 mm wide shall pass through a 37.5 mm BS sieve.

S6. Flexible and Composite Roads

S6.1 Reinstatement Methods

The Undertaker shall carry out the reinstatement in accordance with one of the following methods, having regard to the desirability in each case, as appropriate, of carrying out the greatest degree of immediate permanent reinstatement. The permitted materials and layer thicknesses are specified in Appendices A3 and A4.

1) Method A - All Permanent Reinstatement
The entire structure shall be reinstated to a permanent standard at the first visit.

2) Method B - Permanent Basecourse Reinstatement
The basecourse and substructure shall be reinstated to a permanent standard at the first visit. The permanent basecourse material, or an alternative interim material, shall be extended to the surface as the interim wearing course, with or without a thin separating layer of sand at the position of the basecourse/ wearing course interface. On the second visit the interim wearing course shall be removed, typically by cold planing, and a permanent wearing course laid. Where a sand separation layer is present, the sand shall be removed and the surface brushed clean.

3) Method C - Permanent Roadbase Reinstatement
The roadbase and substructure shall be reinstated to a permanent standard at the first visit together with an interim basecourse and wearing course. The interim wearing course and some or all of the interim base course may be a deferred set macadam. The residual portion of the interim base course may be an unbound granular material. On the second visit the interim surfacing shall be removed to the top of the roadbase and a permanent basecourse and wearing course laid.

4) Method D - Permanent Sub-base Reinstatement
The sub-base and substructure shall be reinstated to a permanent standard at the first visit together with an interim granular roadbase and interim surfacing as for Method C. On the second visit the interim reinstatement is removed down to the top of the sub-base and a permanent roadbase, basecourse and wearing course laid.

S6.2 Sub-base Reinstatement

Sub-base reinstatement options are shown in Appendices A3 and A4, subject to the following exceptions:

1) Sub-base Equivalence
The thickness of granular sub-bases may be reduced provided that the thickness of the bituminous basecourse is increased proportionately, in accordance with Section S6.3 (4).

2) Foamed Concrete
A foamed concrete mixture in accordance with Appendix A9 may be laid at sub-base level, regardless of whether the existing sub-base is cement bound.

S6.3 Roadbase Reinstatement

Roadbase reinstatement options are shown in Appendices A3 and A4, subject to the following exceptions:

1) Composite Roads
All composite roads constructed with a roadbase of CBM3, lean-mix concrete or equivalent shall be reinstated with a CBM3 roadbase. The reinstated CBM3 roadbase shall be laid flush with the existing cement-bound roadbase. The total thickness of the reinstated base course and wearing course shall match the existing. The 40 mm wearing course thickness should be maintained by adjustment of the basecourse thickness, wherever practicable.

Continuously reinforced concrete roadbases are not covered by this clause. Special conditions will apply to such reinstatement work and must be agreed with the Authority.

2) Flexible Roads

All other roads, where the existing roadbase is not a cement-bound material, shall be reinstated with a bituminous, granular or other roadbase material that is not cement bound. An exception to this requirement will be permitted in the case of trenches less than 300 mm width or excavations less than 2 square metres, where a CBM3 roadbase, equivalent in thickness to the roadbase of the relevant road type shown in Appendix A4 may be used.

3) Foamed Concrete

A foamed concrete mixture, in accordance with Appendix A9, may be laid at roadbase level, regardless of whether the existing roadbase is cement bound. In Type 1 and 2 flexible roads, a foamed concrete roadbase will be permitted provided that the sub-base is also foamed concrete. Foamed concrete shall not be used, as a permanent reinstatement, within 100 mm of the road surface.

4) Roadbase Equivalence

In Type 3 and 4 flexible roads, the thickness of granular roadbases may be reduced provided that the thickness of the bituminous base course is increased proportionately; each 10 mm increase in bituminous basecourse thickness is considered equivalent to a 35 mm decrease in thickness of DTp Type 1 granular sub-base material at roadbase and/or sub-base levels. This equivalence rule may be applied to any extent, including total replacement of all granular materials at both sub-base and roadbase levels, subject to the following restrictions :

  a) Basecourse and wearing course thicknesses in Type 3 and 4 roads are minimum values and shall not be reduced by application of the 10/35 equivalence of bituminous/granular materials.

  b) Where part of a granular roadbase and/or sub-base is to be replaced by additional basecourse material, the remaining total thickness of granular material at roadbase and/or sub-base level shall not be less than 150 mm.

5) High Sulphate Areas

The Authority shall notify the Undertaker, prior to excavation, of any site where high sulphate levels are known to occur. Following such notification the Undertaker shall incorporate a sulphate resistant cement in all cement-bound materials.

S6.4 Surface Reinstatement

Surface reinstatement options are shown in Appendices A3 and A4, subject to the following :

1) HRA Surface

All roads, where the existing material at the running surface is HRA shall be reinstated with HRA wearing course.

2) Wearing Course Macadam

Where a permanent reinstatement is carried out in Type 3 or 4 roads, a 25 mm thick wearing course of 6 mm dense wearing course macadam may be laid in place of the standard 40 mm thickness, provided the total thickness of basecourse and wearing course is not reduced.

3) Basecourse Macadam

Where a dense bitumen macadam basecourse is to be used as the running surface for a period in excess of 6 months, the target binder content shall be increased by 0.5% above the BS 4987 target value.

4) Small Reinstatements

A permanent wearing course material may be laid in place of a permanent basecourse material in trenches less than 300 mm width or excavations less than 2 square metres. Two 50 mm thick layers may be laid in place of the standard 60 mm and 40 mm thicknesses.

5) Single Course Construction

Where the existing road is of single course construction, permanent basecourse material may be laid up to the surface in place of a separate wearing course, provided that the target binder content is increased by 0.5% above the BS4987 target value.

6) Surface Dressing and Surface Treatments
Where the existing road has a surface dressing or other surface treatment, permanent basecourse material may be laid up to the surface in place of a separate wearing course, and either :

    i)   the target binder of the basecourse shall be increased by 0.5% above the BS4987 target value;

or ii)   the surface dressing or surface treatment shall be reinstated by mutual agreement.

S6.5 Edge Requirements

The edges of excavations may need to be trimmed at wearing course and/or basecourse level, to meet the following requirements :

1) Edge Regularity
All bound edges shall be essentially straight, smooth, vertical and parallel to the line of any trench. All openings shall be "squared off" as necessary to give a reasonably regular plain shape when viewed from above, as shown in Figure S6.1.

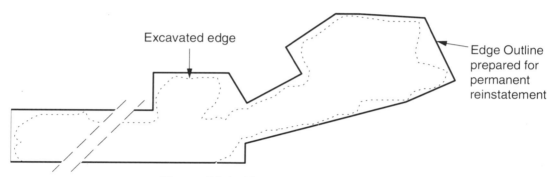

Figure S6.1 - Example of prepared edge

2) Undercutting
All bound edges shall be essentially smooth and vertical with no significant undercutting, as shown in Figure S6.2.

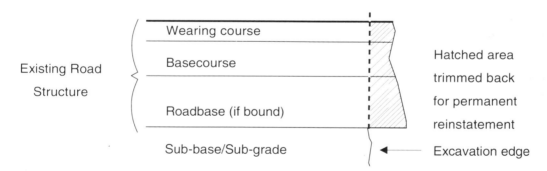

Figure S6.2 - Example of need for trimback

3) Edge Sealing
At any interim stage and at the time of permanent reinstatement all bound vertical edges, kerbs and exposed ironwork shall be painted with a bitumen-based edge sealant or prepared with an equivalent edge sealing system or material. Tack coat solution shall not be used as an edge sealant. There should be no significant spillage, splashing or any deliberate overpainting of the adjacent road surface, subject to the requirements of Section S6.5 (6).

4) Tack Coating
A bitumen-emulsion tack coat solution shall be applied to the surface of the basecourse immediately prior to laying the permanent wearing course, unless the basecourse is newly laid and untrafficked, in which case a tack coat will not be required. The application rate of the tack coat shall be 0.2 to 0.3 litres per square metre unless otherwise recommended by the manufacturer. In the case of small or narrow excavations a bitumen-emulsion edge sealant may be used to provide the tack coat.

5)   Proximity to Road Edges, Ironwork etc.
Where any trim-lines, for edges of excavations, are within 250 mm of the road edge, kerb, other reinstatement or ironwork, the trim-line shall be extended to the interface of such situations. This extra reinstatement may be confined to the wearing course provided lower courses have not been damaged.

6)   Overbanding
Any overbanding or coating of the road surface, at the interface between the existing road and the reinstatement edge, shall not exceed 3 mm thickness nor 40 mm width. The minimum skid resistance value of the material used shall be 55 SRV, as determined by the TRRL Portable Skid-resistance Tester used in accordance with Road Note 27 : 1969

S6.6   Special Materials

1)   Friction Coatings
In the event of notification by the Authority, the permanent reinstatement of sections requiring special friction coatings shall have an agreed, equivalent, surface treatment applied within 10 working days following either the date of completion of the reinstatement, or the date on which the Authority agreed the equivalent treatment, if later.

2)   Coloured Surfacings
Coloured surfacings used to highlight particular highway features shall be restored, subject to the following :

   a) The Authority requests the use of such surfacings at either the planning or notice stage, or, in the event of immediate works, before permanent reinstatement; and
   b) where the local custom and practice has been to complete previous surface restoration using similarly matching surfacings; and
   c) the Authority is able to identify an appropriate source of equivalent coloured surfacings.

3)   Porous Asphalts
In the event of notification by the Authority, the permanent reinstatement of any existing porous asphalt wearing course shall be carried out in accordance with the Authority's requirements

S6.7   Tolerances

1)   Wearing course thicknesses are nominal values with a tolerance of +10 mm to -5 mm. Other layer thicknesses are nominal values with a tolerance of ±10 mm for any bound material and ±20 mm for any unbound material. Where unbound layers are replaced by equivalent bound layers, the tolerances for bound layers shall apply.

2)   The combination of permitted tolerances in the thicknesses of different pavement courses for bitumen and cement bound materials shall not result in a reduction in thickness of the bound pavement, excluding the sub-base, by more than 15 mm from the specified thickness, subject to an absolute minimum 100 mm of bound surfacing in permanent reinstatements.

S7. Rigid and Modular Roads

S7.1 Reinstatement Methods
A rigid road shall be deemed to be a composite road if the total thickness of the existing bituminous overlay exceeds 100mm and reinstated in accordance with Section S6. There shall be no requirement, ordinarily, to replace reinforcement in such a road. However, where it can be shown that such reinforcement is required, and the Authority notifies the Undertaker accordingly, the Undertaker shall provide steel reinforcement in accordance with Section S7.5.

Some modern road constructions incorporating special design philosophies are outside the scope of this specification - refer to NG 7.1.

Reinstatement shall be carried out in accordance with one of the following options. The permitted materials and layer thickness are specified in Appendices A5 and A6.

1) Method A - All Permanent Reinstatement
The backfill, sub-base (if existing), concrete road slab and any existing bituminous surface overlay shall be reinstated to a permanent standard at the first visit.

2) Method B - Permanent Sub-base Reinstatement
The backfill and substructure shall be reinstated to a permanent standard at the first visit together with an interim bituminous wearing course as per Section S6.1, Method D. The lower portion of the concrete road slab and any existing sub-base shall be reinstated, for the interim period, with an unbound material. Alternatively, any existing sub-base may be reinstated immediately to a permanent standard. On the second visit the interim wearing course and underlying interim granular material and any interim sub-base materials shall be removed and a permanent sub-base (if existing), concrete road slab and any bituminous surface overlay reinstated.

S7.2 Sub-base Reinstatement

1) General
In a rigid road the sub-base is deemed to be any layer of imported granular or cement bound material existing immediately below the base of the concrete road slab. Where such a sub-base layer exists, a similar or equivalent material shall be laid to a thickness of 300 mm, or to match the existing, whichever is less.

2) Foamed Concrete
A foamed concrete mixture in accordance with Appendix A9 may be laid at sub-base level, regardless of whether the existing sub-base is cement bound

S7.3 Concrete Road Slab Reinstatement

Road slab reinstatement options are shown in Appendix A5, subject to the following :

1) Concrete Specification
The concrete road slab shall be reinstated using C40 concrete mixed in accordance with SHW Clause 1001, with an air entrainment admixture used in at least the top 50 mm of the road slab. Exceptionally, where mutually agreed by the Authority and Undertaker, an alternative material may be used to suit site conditions, e.g. high early strength mix may be agreed to allow an earlier re-opening of a heavily trafficked road. Where concrete is mixed off site, quality assurance certificates detailing the specifications against which the concrete has been ordered and supplied, shall be obtained by the Undertaker for confirmation of material quality. In the case of excavations less than 2 square metres, a site batched equivalent to C40 concrete may be used.

2) Joints
All contraction, expansion and warping joints that are removed or otherwise damaged during the excavation operation must be replaced or reconstructed to a similar design and using equivalent materials, at the time of permanent reinstatement.

3) Membranes
A slip membrane shall be used beneath the road slab and a curing membrane shall be used above. Impermeable polythene or similar sheeting may be used for both slip and curing membranes; an approved sprayed plastic film may be used as a curing membrane.

4) Opening to Traffic

The cured road slab may be opened to traffic as soon as a crushing strength of 25 N/mm² has been achieved.

S7.4 Edge Requirements

S7.4.1 Edge Support

Support for the edges of the road slab reinstatement shall be provided in accordance with one of the following options :

1) Slab edge taper

Where the surface of the concrete road slab is the running surface of the road, the excavation shall be delineated by pavement saw to a depth of 30 ±10 mm. Other excavations may also be delineated by pavement saw. The remainder of the exposed faces of all road slabs should be roughcut, at an angle of 27 ±18° to the vertical as shown in Figure S7.1.

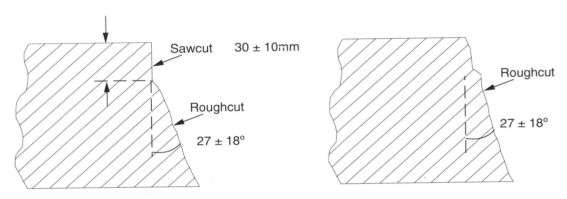

Figure S7.1 - Slab edge taper options

2) Dowel bars

Where the surface of the concrete road slab is the running surface of the road, the excavation shall be delineated by pavement saw to a minimum depth of 20 mm. Other excavations may also be delineated by pavement saw. Any unsawn section of the slab shall be left roughcut to give an essentially vertical face. A series of horizontal holes shall be drilled at the centre depth of the exposed faces, to provide a sliding fit for 20 mm or 25 mm nominal diameter steel dowel bars. The minimum dowel bar length shall be equal to the width of the reinstatement less 50 mm, the maximum dowel bar length shall be 400 mm and the nominal hole depth shall be equal to 50% of the actual dowel bar length ±50 mm. The holes shall be drilled at 600 ±100 mm centres, with holes along one edge of the slab offset or staggered by at least 200 mm when viewed from above, as shown in Figure S7.2.

S7.4.2 Edge Preparation

Any cracking within the adjacent road slab resulting from the excavation operation shall require the relevant area of the slab to be removed and included within the area to be reinstated. The edges of excavations may need to be trimmed over part or all of the thickness of the concrete road slab to meet the following requirements:

1) Edge Regularity

The requirements specified in Section S6.5.1 shall apply.

2) Undercutting

The requirements specified in Section S6.5.2 shall apply.

3) Edge Condition

All edges shall be cleaned and wetted prior to the placement of the concrete.

4) Proximity to Joints, Ironwork etc.

Where, following trimming, the excavation extends to within 300 mm of the edge of the road slab, joint, other reinstatement or ironwork that remainder of the slab shall be removed and included within the area to be reinstated.

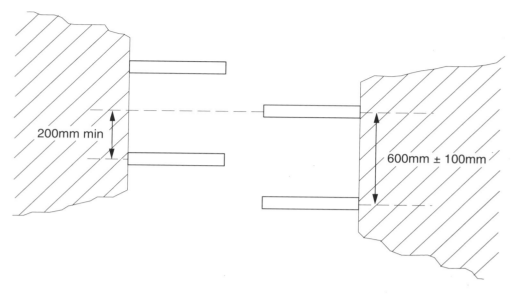

Figure S7.2 - Dowel bar arrangement - Plan view

S7.5 Reinforcement

Where steel reinforcement within the concrete road slab has been cut out, new steel reinforcing mesh of equivalent weight shall be provided. The new reinforcement mesh shall be lapped and wired or welded to the existing reinforcement. A minimum of 150 mm of the existing reinforcement shall be exposed to allow adequate attachment to the new reinforcement. Where 150 mm of the exposed reinforcement cannot be preserved during the excavation it will be necessary to trim back the concrete road slab as required to expose additional reinforcement. This additional trimming shall not supersede the requirement to provide a slab edge taper or dowel bars.

S7.6 Overlays

Where the surface of the concrete road slab is overlaid with a bituminous material, a matching thickness of a similar or equivalent material shall be laid. Such material shall not be laid to a thickness less than that recommended by BS 4987 or BS 594 for the nominal size used for each layer of material laid. Edge preparation shall be carried out in accordance with Section S6.5, except that the existing edge of the overlay shall be trimmed back by a distance equal to the nominal thickness of the overlay, or 40 mm, whichever is the greater.

S7.7 Modular Roads

Reinstatements shall be carried out in accordance with the options, permitted materials and layer thicknesses specified in Appendix A6, subject to the following :

1)   Clean undamaged modules shall be re-used. Where insufficient modules remain for reinstatement use and identical replacements are no longer available, then a reasonably similar colour, shape and size shall be the preferred order of criteria in the choice of acceptable replacements.

2)   Bedding material shall be sand or mortar, to match the existing type and thickness. Sand, mortar or other grouting, to match the existing, shall be applied to gaps between individual blocks at the time of permanent reinstatement.

3)   The sub-base and roadbase layers may be reinstated to match the existing, or its structural equivalent, using materials permitted by Sections S6.2 and S6.3 of this specification.

4)   Where an interim surface reinstatement is required, the existing modules should be reused, including the use of broken modules. Where damage has resulted in fragmentation or widespread breakage of modules, then a cement bound material, deferred set macadam or other cold laid macadam may be used for interim reinstatement provided that compaction of such materials does not result in further damage to adjacent modules.

S8. Footways, Footpaths and Cycletracks

S8.1 Reinstatement Method

The Undertaker shall carry out the reinstatement in accordance with one of the following methods, having regard to the desirability in each case, as appropriate, of carrying out the greatest degree of immediate permanent reinstatement. The permitted materials and layer thicknesses are specified in Appendix A7.

1)   Method A - All Permanent Reinstatement
The sub-base, basecourse and wearing course, or equivalent, shall be reinstated to a permanent standard at the first visit.

2)   Method B - Permanent Basecourse Reinstatement
The sub-base and basecourse shall be reinstated to a permanent standard at the first visit. The permanent basecourse material, or an alternative interim material, shall be extended to the surface as the interim wearing course, with or without a thin separating medium at the position of the basecourse/wearing course interface. On the second visit the interim wearing course shall be removed and the permanent wearing course laid.

3)   Method C - Permanent Sub-Base Reinstatement
The sub-base and substructure shall be reinstated to a permanent standard at the first visit together with an interim, bituminous, basecourse and surfacing. For concrete or bituminous footways, footpaths and cycle-tracks the interim wearing course and some or all of the interim basecourse may be a deferred set macadam. The lower portion of the interim basecourse may be an unbound granular material. For modular footways, footpaths and cycletracks the interim surfacing may be a cold-laid material, paving modules or a combination thereof. On the second visit, the entire interim surfacing shall be removed to the top of the sub-base and a permanent basecourse and wearing course laid.

S8.2 Basecourse and Sub-base Reinstatement

Basecourse and sub-base reinstatement options are shown in Appendix A7, subject to the following exceptions:

1)   General
The sub-base shall be reinstated using similar or equivalent materials to a thickness of 150 mm, or to match the existing, whichever is less, subject to a minimum of 100 mm.

2)   Foamed Concrete
A foamed concrete mixture in accordance with Appendix A9 may be laid at sub-base level, regardless of whether the existing sub-base is cement bound.

S8.3 Surface Reinstatement

Surface reinstatement options are shown in Appendix A7, subject to the following exceptions. Edge preparation shall be carried out in accordance with Sections S6.5 (1) to (6) inclusive, or Section S7.4.2 (1) to (3) inclusive, as appropriate.

1)   High Duty and High Amenity
The Authority shall register all high duty and/or high amenity footways, footpaths or cycletracks and shall identify a suitable source or supplier of reinstatement materials. The Undertaker shall reinstate all registered High Duty/High Amenity footways or footpaths with matching materials from the identified source or supplier. Where aggregates of an especially distinctive colour are encountered, a matching aggregate shall be provided in accordance with Section S6.6 (2).

2)   Other Macadam
Other coated macadam footways, footpaths or cycletracks shall be reinstated using 6 mm size dense wearing course macadam. Where the existing surface is a coated macadam of aggregate size significantly finer than 6 mm nominal size, then the footway or footpath may be regarded as macadam or as asphalt, at the option of the Undertaker, and reinstated accordingly.

3) Other Asphalt

Other asphalt footways, footpaths or cycletracks shall be reinstated using a 15/10 hot rolled asphalt, chipped as necessary to match the existing. Where the existing material is mastic asphalt, asphalt carpet, sand carpet or other derivative, 15/10 hot rolled asphalt shall still be used.

4) Other Concrete

In general reinstatements in a concrete footway, footpath or cycletrack should match the existing surfacing as closely as is practicable. In all cases C30 minimum strength concrete or, for small excavations a site batched concrete of equivalent strength, shall be laid to match the existing thickness. Air entrained concrete to SHW Clause 1001 shall be used wherever the existing concrete has been air entrained, and may be used elsewhere at the discretion of the Undertakers.

5) Modular Footways or Footpaths

i)   Undamaged modules shall be re-used. Where insufficient modules remain for reinstatement use and identical replacements are no longer available, then a reasonably similar colour, shape and size shall be the preferred order of criteria in the choice of acceptable replacements.

ii)   Bedding material shall be sand or mortar, to match the existing type and thickness. Sand, mortar or other grouting, to match the existing, shall be applied to gaps between individual blocks at the time of permanent reinstatement.

iii)   Where an interim surface reinstatement is required, the existing modules should be reused, including the use of broken modules. Where damage has resulted in fragmentation or widespread breakage of modules, then a cement bound material, deferred set macadam or other cold laid macadam may be used for interim reinstatement provided that compaction of such materials does not result in further damage to adjacent modules.

iv)   Where the existing surface has settled and/or is badly broken over a relatively large area extending substantially more than one module width beyond the limits of the Undertakers' works, there will be difficulty in providing a consistent and adequate standard of reinstatement throughout the damaged area without incurring hazardous trips at the interface between the existing and reinstated surfaces. In such cases, the area of surface reinstatement shall be extended to include the entire area of settled or broken surfacing, with an appropriate apportionment of costs between the Undertaker and Authority. Whenever the area of permanent reinstatement needs to be extended to include an existing area of settled or broken modular surfacing, the Undertaker shall notify the Authority prior to excavation.

v)   A joint inspection shall be arranged prior to the commencement of works, to agree the extent of the settled or broken surfacing and to agree an apportionment of costs based on the relative area of permanent reinstatement. In the event of any Authority failing to attend a joint inspection or reach agreement prior to the commencement of the works, the area of settled or broken surfacing shall be completed to an interim standard. Permanent reinstatement may be delayed until such time as the Undertaker is able to recover the relevant proportion of costs from the Authority. At the completion of the works the Undertaker shall recover all agreed costs from the Authority.

S8.4 Commercial Vehicle Access

Where a recognised route for commercial vehicles crosses a footway, footpath or cycletrack, or specified pedestrian area, it shall be assumed that provisions for vehicle loading were incorporated in the original design. Reinstatements of such areas shall be considered as sections of Type 4 roads, of flexible, composite or rigid construction, dependent on the existing construction, and reinstated in accordance with Section S6 or S7 as appropriate. Where a special construction has been incorporated within the original design to cater for expected traffic greater than the Type 4 limiting capacity, the Undertaker should consult the Authority.

S8.5 Domestic Vehicle Access

Where there is a recognised domestic vehicle crossing or occasional emergency service vehicle access across a footway, footpath or cycletrack, specified pedestrian area or precinct, one or more layers within the structure may have been strengthened by the use of thicker layers, higher quality materials or additional modular sections. Reinstatements of such areas shall match the existing layer thicknesses with similar or equivalent materials.

S8.6 Excavations Adjacent to Roads

Where road construction layers, foundation platforms, structural course, kerb beams and backing etc providing edge support to the road structure are found to extend below an adjacent footway, footpath, cycletrack or verge, any reinstatement therein shall take account of such provisions. In such cases, the sub-structure of the footway, footpath, cycletrack or verge shall be reinstated to match the existing layer thicknesses with similar or equivalent materials.

S9. Verges

1) All backfill materials shall comply with the requirements of Section S5.

2) Grassed areas shall be reinstated using the original turf, replacement turf or an equivalent seed, depending on weather and growing season. In all cases, a reasonable growth shall be established within the following 12 months. Within previously mown areas, the surface shall be left free from stones greater than 20 mm nominal size.

3) Any shrubs, trees or planted areas shall be reinstated with the same species, unless otherwise agreed, and shall be established within the following 12 months.

4) Existing top soil within 200 mm of the surface shall be kept separate for subsequent re-use. Alternatively, an imported top soil may be used to a depth of 100 mm or to match the existing depth of top soil, whichever is less.

5) Where road construction layers have been incorporated within the verge, providing edge support to the road structure, the reinstatement shall comply with the requirements of Section S8.6.

6) Verges, ditches and drainage courses shall be restored to their original profile, unless otherwise agreed.

S10. Compaction

All materials laid more than 250 mm above the crown of the Undertakers' apparatus shall be compacted to the following overall requirements .

S10.1 Cohesive Materials

All Class D cohesive materials shall be compacted in accordance with Appendix A8.

S10.2 Granular Materials

All Class C cohesive/granular materials, Class B granular materials, Class A graded granular materials and all cement-bound granular materials shall be compacted in accordance with Appendix A8.

S10.3 Bituminous Materials

All coated macadams, asphalts and other bituminous materials, shall be compacted in accordance with Appendix A8.

S10.4 Concretes

All pavement quality concrete laid as the surface slab of road, footway, footpath or cycletrack reinstatements, shall be compacted using a proprietary vibrator, selected and operated in accordance with the manufacturer's recommendations, subject to the following exceptions :.

1)   Small Reinstatements
Proprietary vibrators may be unsuitable for concrete sections less than 100 mm wide or less than 0.5 square metres in area. In such cases, all concrete shall be thoroughly tamped.

2)   Foamed Concrete
Foamed concretes shall not be tamped, or otherwise compacted, unless specifically required, and then in accordance with the manufacturer's recommendations.

S10.5 Modular Surfacing Materials

If compaction is required, equipment shall be operated in accordance with the manufacturer's instructions.

S10.6 Equipment Operation and Restrictions

Refer to Section NG10.6 and Appendix A.8.

S11. Ancillary Activities

S11.1 Test Holes

1) *25 mm Diameter or Less*
Holes shall be reinstated using a fine aggregate, bound with cement or cold bitumen for the upper layers, and compacted in layers up to 100 mm thickness to finish flush with the surface. Alternatively, a flexible sealing plug may be installed flush with the surface.

2) *25 mm to 100 mm Diameter*
Holes shall be reinstated using a fine aggregate, compacted in layers up to 100 mm thickness. An appropriate cement-bound, cold-laid or hot-laid bituminous material shall be compacted to finish flush with the paved surface. Its thickness shall be the same as the concrete or bituminous thickness required by the specification for that road category.

3) *Greater than100 mm Diameter*
Holes shall be reinstated using a Class A graded granular material, placed in layers up to 100 mm thickness and compacted using mechanical plant. An appropriate cement-bound, cold-laid or hot-laid bituminous material shall be compacted to finish flush with the paved surface. Its thickness shall be the same as the concrete or bituminous thickness required by the specification for that road category. Within flexible road surfaces, the reinstatement shall be subject to the edge sealing requirements of S6.5 (3).

S11.2 Street Furniture, Special Features, etc.

1) Traffic signs or road markings removed during the course of works shall be replaced in an equivalent material, to the original width and spacing, immediately following completion of the works.

2) Temporary road markings may be applied during the interim period, using a quick drying durable paint, adhesive strip or similar, and shall similarly be permitted for up to 10 working days immediately following the completion of the permanent reinstatement.

3) Street furniture and special road features such as tactile paving removed during the course of works shall be replaced immediately following completion of the works. This requirement must be met for both interim and permanent reinstatements.

S11.3 Traffic Sensors etc

Where excavation is planned at or near to traffic sensors, advice regarding precautions to avoid damage shall be sought from the relevant Authority before work commences.

S11.4 Sewers, Drains or Tunnels

1) An undertaker executing street works which involve breaking up or opening a sewer, drain or tunnel shall reinstate it to the reasonable requirements and satisfaction of the responsible authority.

2) For this purpose, the "responsible authority" means, in the case of a public sewer, the sewerage undertaker (ie the water service company for the relevant area), and in the case of any other sewer, drain or tunnel, the owner or the person (or authority or body) having the management or control of it.

S12. Remedial Works

The Undertaker is responsible for ensuring that reinstatements comply with the required performance criteria throughout the interim reinstatement and guarantee periods. When determining whether a reinstatement requires any remedial action, the quality of the reinstatement shall be assessed relative to the condition of the adjacent surfaces.

S12.1 Safety Requirements

Should a reinstatement fail any safety requirements of this specification, the surface shall be restored to comply with such requirements, in accordance with Section 71 (for England and Wales) or Section 130 (for Scotland) of the New Roads and Street Works Act 1991.

S12.2 Repair of Cracking

Interface cracks, open by more than 2.5 mm for more than 1 metre of continuous length, or for more than 10% of the perimeter, whichever is the greater, shall require remedial action. In the case of excavations less than 2 square metres, cracks open by more than 2.5 mm for more than 500 mm total length shall require remedial action. Cracks, remote from the reinstatement interface, open by more than 2.5 mm for more than 2 metres of continuous length shall also require remedial action, provided it can reasonably be shown that such cracks occurred directly as a result of the Undertakers' works.

Excessive cracking shall be repaired as follows:

1) Cracks of between 2.5 mm and 10 mm width shall be repaired by filling with a flexible bituminous sealant, subject to the requirements of Section S6.5.(6).

2) Cracks over 10 mm wide shall be repaired by filling with a flexible bituminous sealant incorporating a suitable fine aggregate filler, subject to the requirements of Section S6.5.(6).

3) A maximum of two resealing operations, excluding the original sealing operation, shall be permitted during the guarantee period. Excessive cracking of the third seal shall require a surface repair operation, as follows:

  i) Removal of the surface material to the full depth of the wearing course or to 40 mm depth, whichever is less; for the full length of the crack or for 1 metre length, whichever is greater.

  ii) The surface shall be removed over sufficient width to ensure that the repair patch extends beyond the edges of the crack, by a minimum distance equal to the nominal thickness of the replacement wearing course. The minimum width of the repair strip shall be 100 mm.

  iii) Where such a crack repair is required within 300 mm of any other such repair, the intermediate area shall be included in the repair.

  iv) The replacement wearing course patch shall be laid in accordance with Section S6.4.

  v) If the crack extends into the basecourse layer, the affected materials shall be removed and replaced in accordance with Section S6.4.

S12.3 Repair of Settlement Beyond Reinstatement Limits

Where significant settlement of the surface beyond the edges of the reinstatement can reasonably be shown to have occurred as a direct result of the Undertaker's works, the effective width of the reinstatement shall be deemed to be the actual width of the settled area. The relevant requirements of this specification shall apply over the revised width of the reinstatement. The extent of any significant settlement beyond the reinstatement limits shall be assessed, by mutual agreement, from consideration of the following :

  1) the apparent extent of any excessive areas of standing water following heavy rainfall, or

2) the apparent extent of any significant deterioration of highway shape compared with the existing profile remote from the excavation, or

3) the true extent of any significant deterioration of highway shape determined by profile measurements taken before and after the Undertaker's works.

S12.4 Repair of Other Significant Defects

The requirement for and extent of any repair shall be determined, by mutual agreement, from a consideration of the existing and adjacent surfaces. Where it can reasonably be shown that a repair operation is required, as a direct result of the Undertaker's works, the Undertaker shall carry out remedial actions, as necessary.

Appendix A1

Backfill Materials

A1.1 Class A - Graded Granular Materials

1) Material shall, at the time of compaction, be at an appropriate moisture content between +1% and -2% of the optimum moisture content as determined by BS1377 : Part 4; Vibrating Hammer Method, Method 3.7, or shall be acceptable when subjected to field identification test No.3.

2) Material shall show a 10% fines value of 40 kN or more, as determined in accordance with BS812: Part III, tested in the soaked condition. The principal materials that will be excluded are sandstones, weakly cemented gritstones, the softer magnesium limestones, oolitic limestones and the majority of chalks. Man-made aggregates , e.g. slag, pfa's, clinkers and bottom furnace ash will need individual assessment; it is possible to demonstrate satisfactory performance with some of these materials, even when they fail to meet the 10% fines value requirement.

A1.2 Class B - Granular Materials

Material shall, at the time of compaction, be at an appropriate moisture content between +1% and -2% of the optimum moisture content as determined by BS1377 : Part 4; Vibrating Hammer Method, Method 3.7, or shall be acceptable when subjected to field identification test No.3.

A1.3 Class C - Cohesive/Granular Materials

1) Materials with less than 50% granular content by weight shall, at the time of compaction, be at an appropriate moisture content between 0.8 and 1.2 times the plastic limit, or be acceptable when subjected to field identification test No.2.

2) Materials with a minimum of 50% granular content by weight shall, at the time of compaction, be at an appropriate moisture content between +1% and -2% of the optimum moisture content as determined by BS1377 : Part4; Vibrating Hammer Method, Method 3.7, or shall be acceptable when subjected to field identification test No.3.

A1.4 Class D - Cohesive Materials

1) The moisture content, shall at the time of compaction, be at an appropriate value between 0.8 and 1.2 times the plastic limit, or be acceptable when subjected to field identification test No.2.

2) Clays that contain insufficient moisture when excavated, or that have dried excessively during site storage, as defined by field identification test No. 2, may be re-used provided they are wetted and/or compacted as agreed with the Authority.

3) High silt content materials, as defined by field identification test No. 1, shall be compacted in accordance with Appendix A8 requirements for Class D cohesive materials.

A1.5 Class E - Unacceptable Materials

The following materials, listed as unacceptable in SHW Clause 601 paragraphs 2(ii) and 3 , shall not be used at any level within the permanent structure of any reinstatement :

1) Peat and materials from swamps, marshes or bogs.

2) Logs, stumps and perishable materials.

3) Materials in a frozen condition. (Such materials, if otherwise suitable, shall be classified as suitable when unfrozen.)

4) Clays having a liquid limit exceeding 90, determined in accordance with BS1377 : Part 2 Method 4, or a Plasticity Index exceeding 65, determined in accordance BS1377 : Part 2 Method 5.4.

5) Materials susceptible to spontaneous combustion.

6) Materials having hazardous chemical or physical properties requiring special measures for its excavation, handling, storage, transportation, deposition and disposal.

A1.6. Field Identification Tests

The following identification tests must be carried out immediately prior to the placement and compaction of the backfill material.

Test 1   Silt Identification

High silt content materials can usually be identified by selecting a moist sample of the fine material only and carrying out a simple hand test:

> With clean dry hands, rub the sample between the palms, remove the excess material by striking the palms together and wait a few minutes for body heat to dry out any material adhering to the hands. Finally, rub hands together briskly. If no significant quantity of material remains adhering to the palms, i.e. the palms are relatively clean, then the sample tested is essentially a silt. The proportion of granular material discarded to produce the fine sample needs to be taken into account.

Test 2   Clay Condition

Clays suitable for compaction with pedestrian controlled compaction plant can usually be identified by selecting a sample of small lumps of the fine material only, at a moisture content representative of the bulk material, and carrying out a simple roll test:

> With clean dry hands, take the sample and squeeze together in one hand and release. If the sample crumbles away and mostly fails to hold together into a 'ball' then the sample is too dry for compaction. If not, break off part of the ball and roll between the palms or between one palm and any convenient clean dry flat surface, for example the back of a spade. Roll out the sample into a long thin cylinder until it fractures or begins to show significant transverse cracks. If the strand can be rolled into intact or uncracked lengths that are thinner or longer than a standard pencil, i.e. much less than around 7 mm diameter or substantially more than around 175 mm length then the sample is too wet or too plastic for compaction. Any result between the ball and the pencil is acceptable for use provided the bulk of the material consists of lumps less than 75 mm in size.

Test 3   Granular Condition

All granular materials must be compacted near to their optimum moisture content which can vary considerably depending on the average particle size and, to a much smaller extent, on the type of mineral or rock involved. However, a laboratory compaction test is invariably carried out on a sample of material from which the larger particles have been removed, the sample is always compacted in a small smooth-sided steel cylinder and the standard methods of compaction bear little similarity with current compaction plant. Experience has shown that the most commonly specified laboratory compaction test ie. BS1377 : Part 4; Vibrating Hammer Method, Method 3.7 will produce an optimum moisture content result that is, typically, significantly wetter than the field optimum for a granular material that is to be compacted within a trench using a vibrotamper.

Granular materials suitable for compaction by pedestrian controlled plant can usually be identified by a simple visual examination. Typically, the test will identify materials within 1% to 1.5% of the field optimum moisture content depending on the mineral type. Experience has shown that compaction within this visual moisture range will not normally show any significant reduction in compaction performance. The test cannot indicate the actual moisture content of any material but this is rarely of any relevance as far as an operator is concerned.

Depending on the size of the stockpile, dig out representative samples from beneath the outer surface at several positions around the outside and examine several of the medium and larger sized particles from each sample extracted:

Material within the target moisture content range will show a dull sheen when viewed obliquely against the light, with all fines adhering to the larger particles, and no free water will be visible. Material at the dry limit will not show the characteristic sheen, fines will not be strongly adherent and many of the fines will be free. Material at the wet limit will begin to show free moisture collecting in surface grooves or amongst the fines, fines will not be strongly adherent and many of the fines will amalgamate as soggy clusters. Any result between the wet and dry limits is acceptable provided the bulk of the sample is reasonably well graded.

Sands used as finefill or as a regulating layer also need to be used near to the optimum moisture content and can be identified by a simple squeeze test. Take a small sample of representative sand, squeeze in one hand and release. If the sample crumbles away and mostly fails to adhere together into a 'ball' then the sample is too dry. Any reasonable degree of adherence is acceptable provided no free water is squeezed out.

Test 4   Granular Grading

All unbound granular materials must be reasonably well graded, ie. must contain a range of particle sizes, from fine to coarse, with an adequate proportion of particles of intermediate sizes. A well graded material can be compacted to give a dense and stable structure of interlocking particles with a low proportion of air voids within the structure.

Depending on the size of the stockpile, dig out representative samples from beneath the outer surface at several positions around the outside and spread out each sample.

Class A graded granular materials should not contain any particles greater than 75 mm nominal size and, in general, should be 50 mm or smaller. Smaller particles down to less than 5 mm nominal size should be present in gradually increasing numbers as the size decreases. Finer particles, from sand size down to dust, should be present and will usually be adhering to the larger particles. Fine particles should be visible adhering to around 30 per cent or more of the surface of the majority of the larger particles.

Class B granular materials should show the same general features as described above but will usually be less well graded overall compared with Class A graded granular materials.

Class C cohesive/granular material will usually contain a much larger proportion of fine material. The granular content should still be less than 75 mm nominal size, down to less than 5 mm nominal size and should not be single sized.

Appendix A2 - Key to Materials

HRAWC – Hot rolled asphalt wearing course to BS 594: Part 1 1985. All roads – 30/14 Design Type F mix, 50 pen (2 to 8 stability) to Table 3, Column 9. Types 2, 3 and 4 roads – 30/14 Recipe Type F mix, 50 pen to Table 5, Column 21. Footways – 15/10 Recipe Type F mix to Table 5, Column 19.

CGWC – Close graded wearing course macadam to BS 4987: Part 1 1988. All roads – 10mm size close graded, 100 pen to Clause 7.4.

DBWC – Dense wearing course macadam to BS 4987: Part 1 1988. Types 3 and 4 roads – 6mm size dense, to Clause 7.5. Footways – 6mm size close graded, 100 pen to Clause 7.5.

HRABC – Hot rolled asphalt basecourse to BS 594: Part 1 1985. All roads – 50/20 mix, 50 pen to Table 2, Column 3. Footways – 50/20 mix to Table 2, Column 3.

DBC – Dense basecourse macadam to BS 4987: Part 1 1988. All roads – 20mm size dense, 100 pen to Clause 6.5. Footways – 20mm size dense, to Clause 6.5.

PCWC / PCBC – In accordance with Appendix A10.

DSM – Deferred set macadam 20mm basecourse or 10mm or 6mm wearing course macadam to BS 4987: Part 1 1988 minimum binder viscosity of 30 secs STV – approximately equivalent to 10 days deferred.

Concrete – to SHW Clause 1001. All roads – C40 mix. Footways – C30 mix.

CBM 3 – Cement Bound Material Category 3 to SHW Clause 1038.

GSB 1 – Granular Sub-base Material Type 1 to SHW Clause 803 used in accordance with Appendix A1.

Notes on HRAWC

1. Natural gravels not permitted as coarse aggregate in HRAWC for use in Type 1 and 2 roads.

2. A design mix may give better performance where queuing of heavy traffic is likely to occur. Also, a design mix may be more economical and easier to lay, compact and provide with surface chippings.

3. Chippings shall be 20mm or 14mm nominal size, pre-coated.

Note on Appendices A3 to A7 – All layer thicknesses in millimetres.

BACKFILL MATERIALS

Class A – Class A Graded Granular*

Class B – Class B Granular*

Class C – Class C Cohesive Granular*

Class D – Class D Cohesive*

*used in accordance with Appendix A1.

| Appendix A2 | KEY TO MATERIALS |

41

Appendix A3 - Reinstatement - Flexible Roads

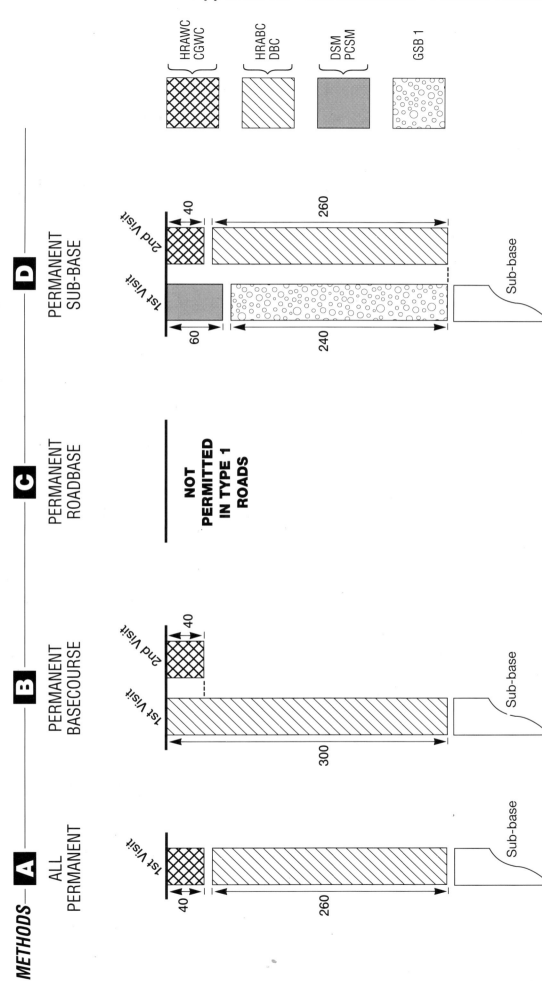

METHODS

A — ALL PERMANENT

B — PERMANENT BASECOURSE

C — PERMANENT ROADBASE

D — PERMANENT SUB-BASE

Legend:
- HRAWC CGWC
- HRABC DBC
- DSM PCSM
- GSB 1

A — ALL PERMANENT
- 1st Visit
- 40
- 260
- Sub-base

B — PERMANENT BASECOURSE
- 2nd Visit: 40
- 1st Visit
- 300
- Sub-base

C — PERMANENT ROADBASE

NOT PERMITTED IN TYPE 1 ROADS

D — PERMANENT SUB-BASE
- 2nd Visit: 40
- 260
- 1st Visit: 60
- 240
- Sub-base

NOTES: 1) Sub-base in accordance with Appendix A3.5
2) For foamed concrete refer to Appendix A9

Appendix A3.1   TYPE 1   FLEXIBLE ROADS

43

METHODS

A ALL PERMANENT

1st Visit

40
210

Sub-base

B PERMANENT BASECOURSE

2nd Visit
1st Visit

40
250

Sub-base

C PERMANENT ROADBASE

NOT PERMITTED IN TYPE 2 ROADS

D PERMANENT SUB-BASE

2nd Visit
1st Visit

40
210
50
200

Sub-base

HRAWC
CGWC
PCWC

HRABC
DBC

DSM
PCSM

GSB 1

NOTES: 1) Sub-base in accordance with Appendix A3.5
2) For foamed concrete refer to Appendix A9

Appendix A3.2 **TYPE 2** **FLEXIBLE ROADS**

44

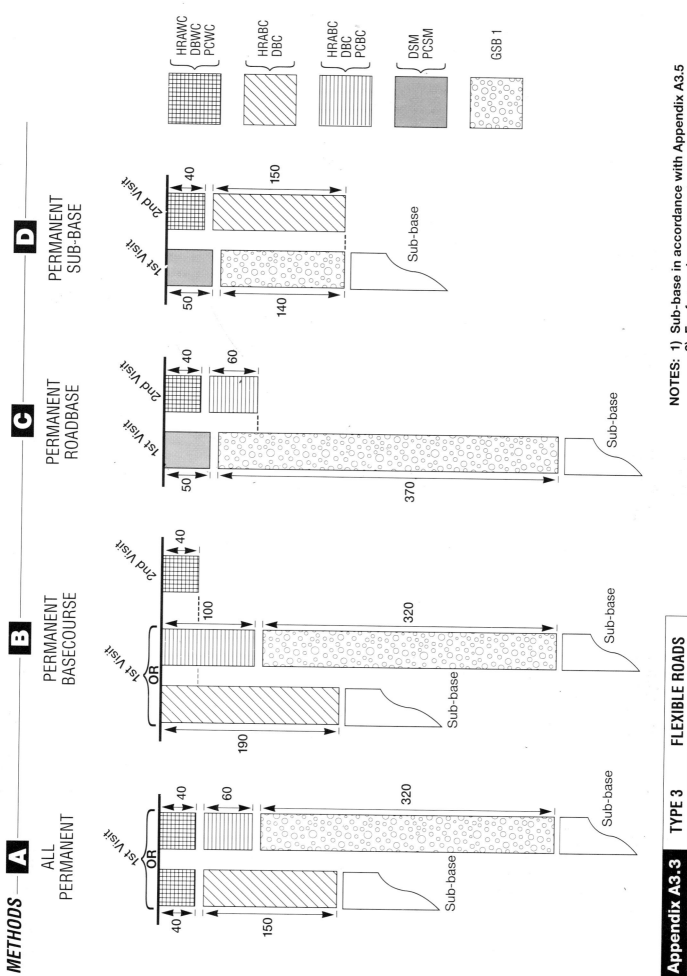

METHODS

A — ALL PERMANENT

B — PERMANENT BASECOURSE

C — PERMANENT ROADBASE

D — PERMANENT SUB-BASE

HRAWC
DBWC
PCWC

HRABC
DBC

HRABC
DBC
PCBC

DSM
PCSM

GSB 1

NOTES: 1) Sub-base in accordance with Appendix A3.5
2) For foamed concrete refer to Appendix A9

Appendix A3.3   TYPE 3   FLEXIBLE ROADS

45

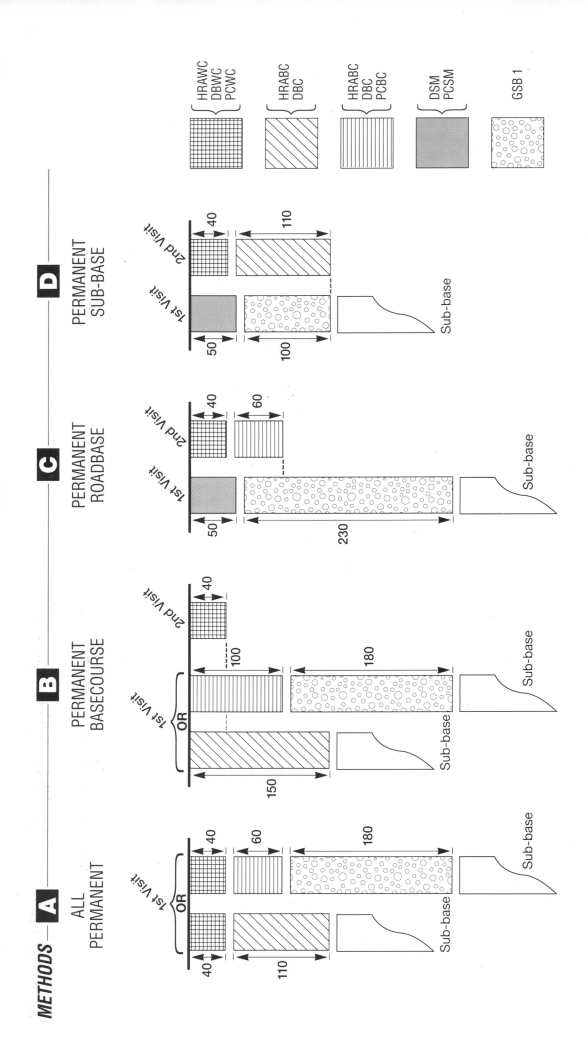

METHODS

A — ALL PERMANENT

B — PERMANENT BASECOURSE

C — PERMANENT ROADBASE

D — PERMANENT SUB-BASE

HRAWC / DBWC / PCWC

HRABC / DBC

HRABC / DBC / PCBC

DSM / PCSM

GSB 1

NOTES: 1) Sub-base in accordance with Appendix A3.5
2) For foamed concrete refer to Appendix A9

Appendix A3.4   **TYPE 4**   **FLEXIBLE ROADS**

46

BACKFILL

CLASS D COHESIVE

CLASS C COHESIVE/GRANULAR

CLASS B GRANULAR

CLASS A GRADED GRANULAR

HRABC DBC

GSB 1

CLASS A

CLASS B

CLASS C

CLASS D

40

60

70

85

OR

*150

*200

*250

*300

* Class A Graded Granular material is permitted alternative

NOTE: For foamed concrete refer to Appendix A9

Appendix A3.5 | **SUB-BASE CONSTRUCTION – FLEXIBLE ROADS**

Appendix A4 - Reinstatement : Composite Roads

Legend:
- HRAWC / CGWC
- HRABC / DBC
- DSM / PCSM
- CBM 3
- GSB 1

METHODS

A — ALL PERMANENT
B — PERMANENT BASECOURSE
C — PERMANENT ROADBASE
D — PERMANENT SUB-BASE

NOTES: 1) Sub-base in accordance with Appendix A4.4
2) For foamed concrete refer to Appendix A9

Appendix A4.1 **TYPE 1** **COMPOSITE ROADS**

49

METHODS

A ALL PERMANENT

B PERMANENT BASECOURSE

C PERMANENT ROADBASE

D PERMANENT SUB-BASE

Legend:
- HRAWC CGWC PCWC
- HRABC DBC
- DSM PCSM
- CBM 3
- GSB 1

* Roadbase to be 250 thick if existing exceeds 200

NOTES: 1) Sub-base in accordance with Appendix A4.4
2) For foamed concrete refer to Appendix A9

| Appendix A4.2 | TYPE 2 | COMPOSITE ROADS |

50

METHODS

A ALL PERMANENT

B PERMANENT BASECOURSE

C PERMANENT ROADBASE

D PERMANENT SUB-BASE

HRAWC
DBWC
PCWC

HRABC
DBC
PCBC

DSM
PCSM

CBM 3

GSB 1

NOTES: 1) Sub-base in accordance with Appendix A4.5
2) For foamed concrete refer to Appendix A9

Appendix A4.3 **TYPES 3&4** **COMPOSITE ROADS**

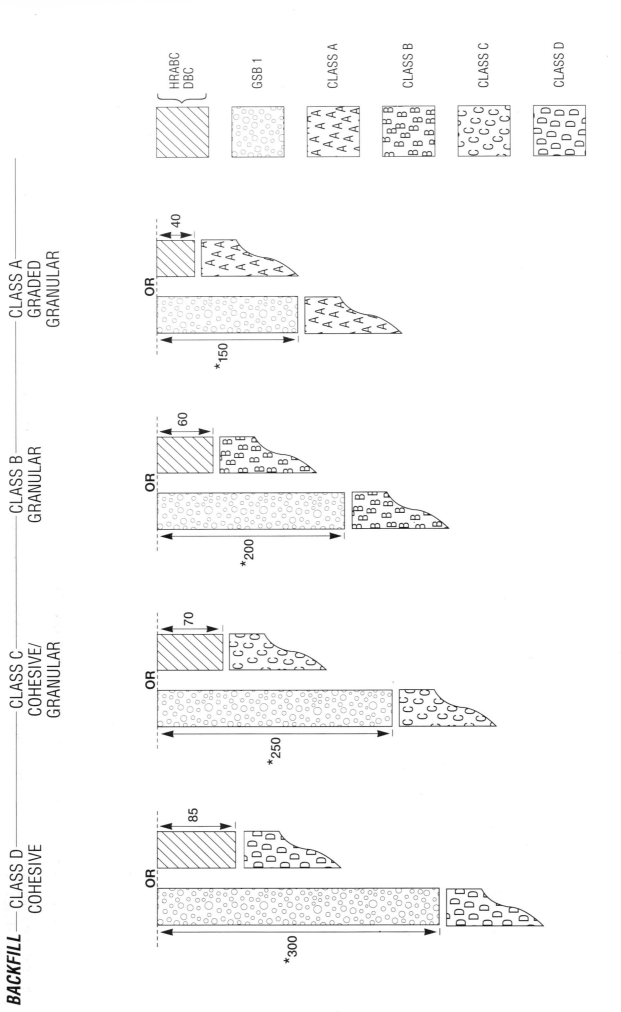

* Class A Graded Granular material is permitted alternative

NOTE: For foamed concrete refer to Appendix A9

Appendix A4.4   SUB-BASE CONSTRUCTION – TYPES 1&2 COMPOSITE ROADS

BACKFILL ── CLASS D
COHESIVE

──── CLASS C ────
COHESIVE/
GRANULAR

──── CLASS B ────
GRANULAR

──── CLASS A ────
GRADED
GRANULAR

HRABC
DBC

GSB 1

CLASS A

CLASS B

CLASS C

CLASS D

40

OR

*150

40

OR

*150

60

OR

*200

70

OR

*250

* Class A Graded Granular material is permitted alternative

NOTE: For foamed concrete refer to Appendix A9

Appendix A4.5   SUB-BASE CONSTRUCTION – TYPES 3&4 COMPOSITE ROADS

53

Appendix A5 - Reinstatement : Rigid Roads

METHODS

HRAWC
CGWC

HRABC
DBC

DSM
PCSM

Concrete

Class A

B

PERMANENT SUB-BASE

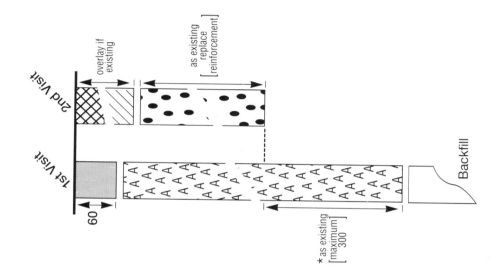

2nd Visit

overlay if existing

as existing replace [reinforcement]

1st Visit

60

* as existing [maximum 300]

Backfill

A

ALL PERMANENT

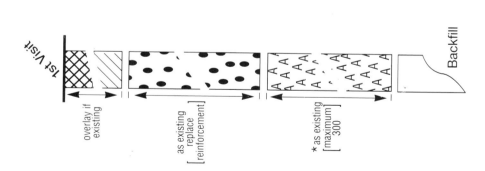

1st Visit

overlay if existing

as existing replace [reinforcement]

* as existing [maximum 300]

Backfill

NOTE: For foamed concrete refer to Appendix A9

* CBM 3 if existing

| Appendix A5.1 | TYPE 1 | RIGID ROADS |

METHODS

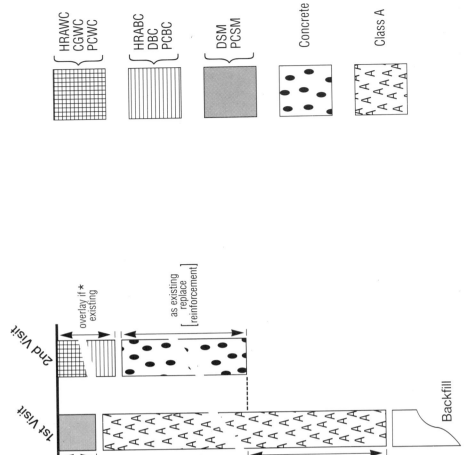

HRAWC
CGWC
PCWC

HRABC
DBC
PCBC

DSM
PCSM

Concrete

Class A

A ALL PERMANENT

B PERMANENT SUB-BASE

1st Visit

2nd Visit

overlay if *
existing

as existing
replace
[reinforcement]

50

**as existing
[maximum 300]

Backfill

* overlay if
existing

as existing
replace
[reinforcement]

** as existing
[maximum 300]

Backfill

NOTE: For foamed concrete refer to Appendix A9

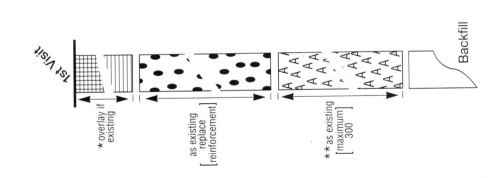

* PCBC not permitted in Type 2 roads

** CBM 3 if existing

| Appendix A5.2 | TYPES 2, 3 & 4 | RIGID ROADS |

56

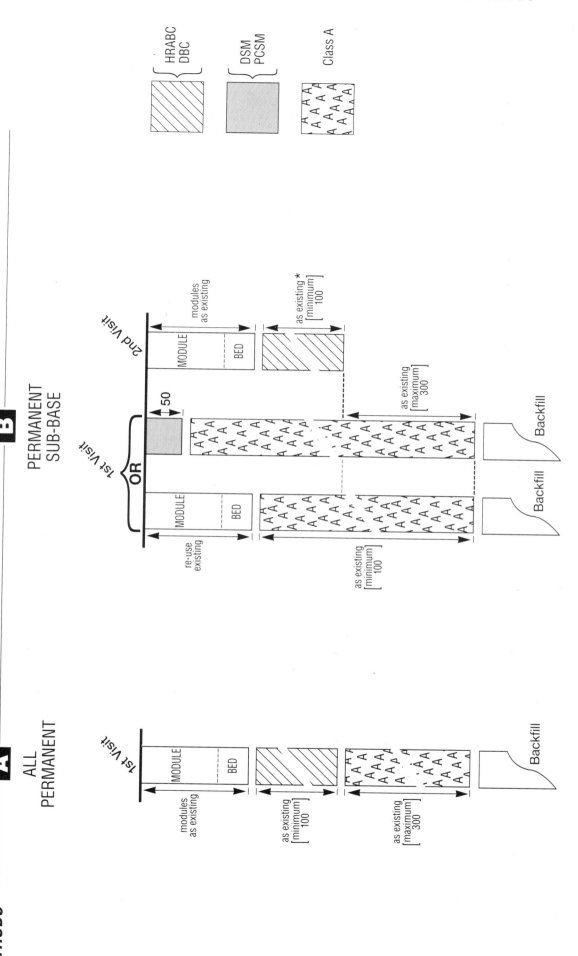

METHODS

A ALL PERMANENT

B PERMANENT SUB-BASE

HRABC
DBC

DSM
PCSM

Class A

1st Visit

MODULE

BED

modules as existing

as existing [minimum 100]

as existing [maximum 300]

Backfill

2nd Visit

MODULE

BED

modules as existing

as existing * [minimum 100]

50

1st Visit

OR

MODULE

BED

re-use existing

as existing [minimum 100]

as existing [maximum 300]

Backfill

Backfill

* May be permanently reinstated on 1st Visit

NOTE: For foamed concrete refer to Appendix A9

| **Appendix A6.1** | **TYPES 3 & 4** | **MODULAR ROADS – Bituminous Roadbase** |

METHODS

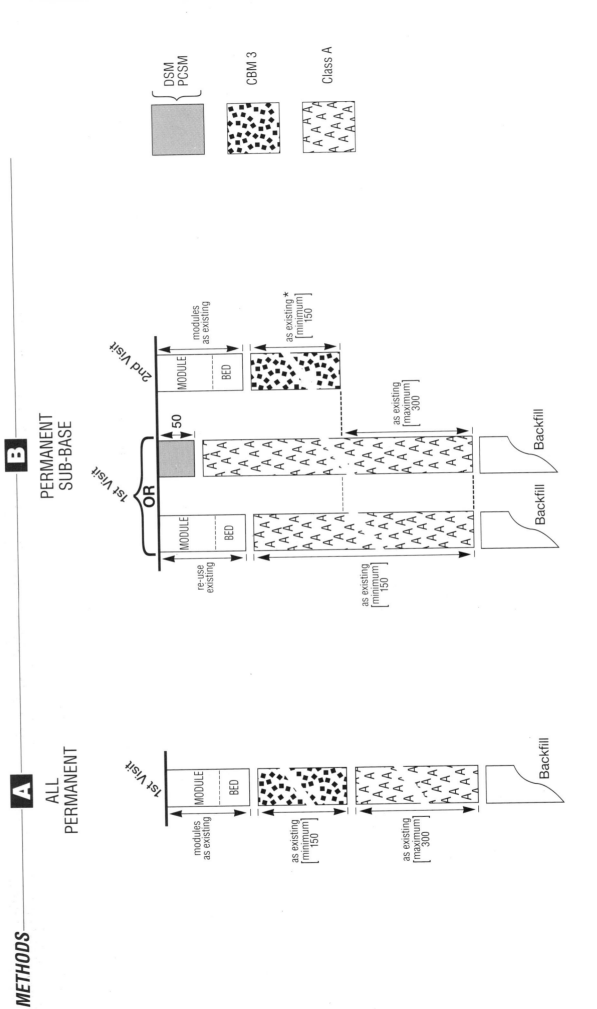

A ALL PERMANENT

B PERMANENT SUB-BASE

1st Visit

MODULE
BED
modules
as existing

as existing
[minimum 150]

as existing
[maximum 300]

Backfill

2nd Visit

MODULE
BED
modules
as existing

as existing *
[minimum 150]

1st Visit

OR

50

MODULE
BED
re-use
existing

as existing
[minimum 150]

as existing
[maximum 300]

Backfill

Backfill

DSM
PCSM

CBM 3

Class A

NOTE: For foamed concrete refer to Appendix A9

* May be permanently reinstated on 1st Visit

| **Appendix A6.2** | **TYPES 3 & 4** | **MODULAR ROADS – Composite Roadbase** |

58

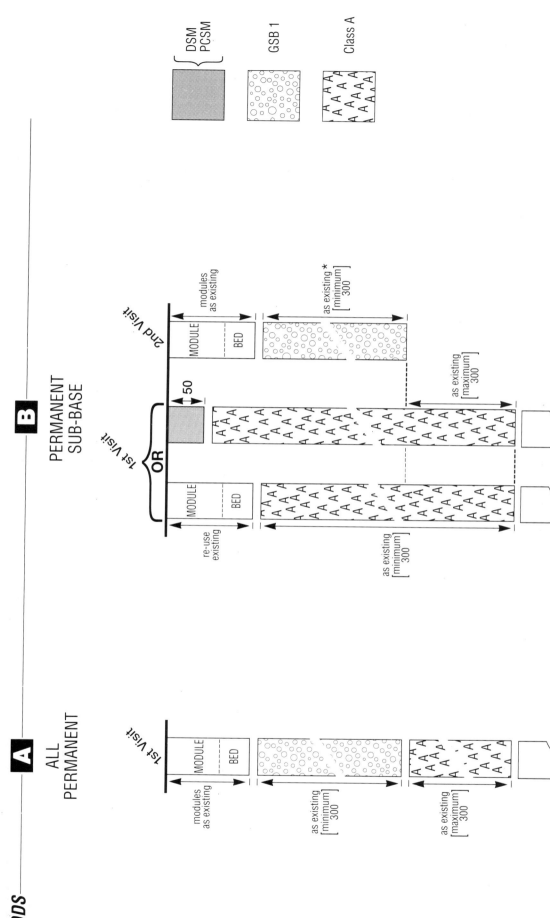

DSM
PCSM

GSB 1

Class A

A ALL PERMANENT

B PERMANENT SUB-BASE

1st Visit

2nd Visit

OR

MODULE

BED

modules as existing

as existing [minimum 300]

as existing [maximum 300]

Backfill

re-use existing

50

as existing * [minimum 300]

as existing [maximum 300]

* May be permanently reinstated on 1st Visit

NOTE: For foamed concrete refer to Appendix A9

Appendix A6.3 | **TYPES 3 & 4** | **MODULAR ROADS – Granular Roadbase**

HRAWC
DBWC
PCWC

HRABC
DBC
PCBC

DSM
PCSM

GSB 1

METHODS

A — ALL PERMANENT

B — PERMANENT BASECOURSE

C — PERMANENT SUB-BASE

1st Visit

2nd Visit

OR

30

50

60

80

Backfill

* as existing [minimum 100]

NOTE: For foamed concrete refer to Appendix A9

* Class A Graded Granular is permitted alternative

Appendix A7.1   **FLEXIBLE FOOTWAYS, FOOTPATHS AND CYCLETRACKS**

61

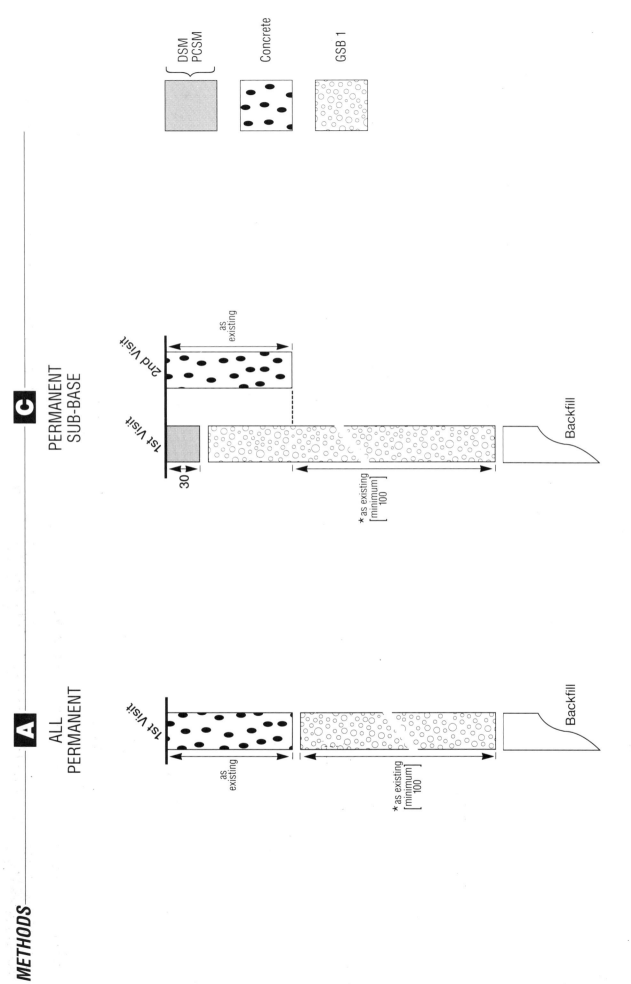

METHODS

A ALL PERMANENT

C PERMANENT SUB-BASE

DSM PCSM

Concrete

GSB 1

1st Visit
as existing
*as existing [minimum 100]
Backfill

2nd Visit
as existing

1st Visit
30
*as existing [minimum 100]
Backfill

* **Class A Graded Granular is permitted alternative**

NOTE: For foamed concrete refer to Appendix A9

Appendix A7.2   **RIGID FOOTWAYS, FOOTPATHS AND CYCLETRACKS**

METHODS

DSM
PCSM

GSB 1

A ALL PERMANENT

1st Visit

MODULE

BED

modules as existing

* as existing [minimum 100]

Backfill

C PERMANENT SUB-BASE

2nd Visit

modules as existing

MODULE

BED

1st Visit

OR

re-use existing

MODULE

BED

as existing * [minimum 100]

Backfill

30

* as existing [minimum 100]

Backfill

* Class A Graded Granular is permitted alternative

NOTE: For foamed concrete refer to Appendix A9

Appendix A7.3   **MODULAR FOOTWAYS, FOOTPATHS AND CYCLETRACKS**

Appendix A8 - Compaction Requirements

Compaction plant and weight category	Cohesive materials (less than 20% granular content) Compaction passes required/Layers of compacted thickness up to:			Granular materials (more than 20% granular content including cement bound granular) Compaction passes required/Layers of compacted thickness up to:			Bituminous materials (all bituminous materials and asphalts) Compaction passes required/Layers of compacted thickness up to:			
	100 mm	150 mm	200 mm	100 mm	150 mm	200 mm	40 mm	60 mm	80 mm	100 mm
Vibrotamper										
50 kg minimum	4	8*	Unsuitable	4	8*	12	5**	7**	9**	12**
Vibrating roller										
600-1000 kg/m single drum	Unsuitable	Unsuitable	Unsuitable	12	Unsuitable	Unsuitable	10	12	Unsuitable	Unsuitable
600-1000 kg/m twin drum	Unsuitable	Unsuitable	Unsuitable	6	12	Unsuitable	5	7	9	12
1000-2000 kg/m single drum	8	Unsuitable	Unsuitable	6	12	Unsuitable	6	10	12	Unsuitable
1000-2000 kg/m twin drum	4	8	Unsuitable	3	6	12	4	5	6	8
2000-3500 kg/m single drum	3	6	9*	3	5	7	5	7	8	12
Over 2000 kg/m twin drum	2	3	5*	2	3	4	3	4	4	6
Over 3500 kg/m single drum	3	4	6*	3	4	6	4	6	7	9
Vibrating plate										
1400-1800 kg/sq.m	Unsuitable	Unsuitable	Unsuitable	5	9	Unsuitable	6	10	12	Unsuitable
Over 1800 kg/sq.m	3	6	9*	3	5	7	4	5	6	8

Cohesive materials notes: Minimum layer thickness 75 mm. * These options are not allowed for use on wholly cohesive materials, i.e pure clay and/or silt containing no particles greater than 75 microns.

Granular materials notes: Minimum layer thickness 75 mm.

Bituminous materials notes: Compaction should be discontinued if any distress to the materials is noticed. (see Notes for Guidance, Section NG 10.3). ** A Vibrotamper shall not be permitted for the compaction of the permanent wearing course applied to trenches of greater than 500 mm width.

Notes :
1) Single drum indicates vibration on one drum only.
2) Twin drum requires vibration on both drums.
3) Twin drum rollers are preferred for bituminous materials.

Alternative plant for trenches less than 200 mm width, small excavations and other areas of restricted access

	Cohesive	Granular	Bituminous
Vibrotamper			
25 kg minimum	6 passes minimum.	6 passes minimum.	6 passes minimum
	Maximum layer thickness 100 mm	Maximum layer thickness 100 mm.	Maximum layer thickness 75 mm.
Percussive rammer			
10 kg minimum	Maximum layer thickness 100 mm	Maximum layer thickness 100 mm.	Maximum layer thickness 75 mm.

Appendix A9

Foamed Concretes for Reinstatement (FCRs)

A9.1 Introduction

Conventional sub-surface reinstatement materials require placement in relatively thin layers, each followed by repeated compaction passes using mechanical vibratory equipment, and the entire process must be replicated several times. The overall procedure is relatively slow, by comparison with excavation and pipe or cable laying activities, and requires additional heavy plant. The use of materials that can be poured into an excavation to the required depth, without compaction of any kind, may allow a more rapid and reliable reinstatement with less dependence on the skill and physical effort of the operators. Such materials have been termed Foamed Concretes for Reinstatement (FCRs) and will incorporate the following basic principles:

1) Adequate strength will be achieved by the use of a chemical binder, e.g. cement, rather than consolidation and mechanical interlocking of aggregate particles.

2) Strength will be controlled by adjustment of the amount of chemical binder addition, the proportion of any aggregate present and the degree of any density adjustment achieved by the entrainment of air or other gases.

3) Mixing may be carried out off-site, adjacent to the reinstatement or within the excavation, using any equipment, adapted as necessary for the manufacture of reinstatement material in quantities appropriate to the intended usage.

4) The overall material performance, and manufacture and placement, are limited only by the need to satisfy the remaining requirements of Appendix A9 of this specification.

A9.2 General Requirements

1) FCRs may be be used in place of other materials, at the discretion of the Undertaker, as follows:

a) At any position within the surround to apparatus and/or backfill layer(s), as the entire layer(s), or combined with any other permitted backfill materials, in any proportion.

b) As a sub-base in any reinstatement, regardless of the materials used above and below.

c) As a combined sub-base and roadbase layer in any reinstatement, regardless of the materials used above and below.

FCRs shall not be used as a permanent reinstatement material above the roadbase level in any road.

2) FCRs shall satisfy the minimum crushing strength, and minimum layer thickness shown in Table A9.1. The maximum crushing strength for all foamed concrete shall not exceed $14N/mm^2$ at 28 days. Where the total foamed concrete laid exceeds 1000 mm thickness, any minimum crushing strength requirement of $4N/mm^2$ shall apply to the top 1000 mm only.

The crushing strength shall be determined, in principle, in accordance with BS1881, with the following exceptions or options :

a) Foamed concrete should not be compacted within the test mould.

b) Test moulds may be 100 mm or 150 mm nominal size; the design and materials etc. of the test mould are not restricted.

c) Storage of samples prior to crush testing is not restricted.

Experience has shown that test results most representative of in-ground conditions are obtained from 150 mm cube samples, prepared using lidded foamed plastic moulds, stored at ambient temperature within the mould.

Layer	Road Type				Footway or Cycletrack
	1	2	3	4	
Roadbase and Sub-base	450 mm C4	450 mm C4	450 mm C2	350 mm C2	N/A
Roadbase alone	Not allowed	Not allowed	300 mm C2	200 mm C2	N/A
Sub-base and/or below	150 mm C2	150 mm C2	150 mm C2	150 mm C2	100 mm C2
C4 - Minimum 4N/mm² crushing strength at 28 days. C2 - Minimum 2N/mm² crushing strength at 28 days.					

Table 9.1 - Layer Thickness and Crushing Strength Requirements

3)   The Authority shall notify the Undertaker, prior to excavation, of any site known to present special drainage or groundwater problems. Following such notification the Undertaker shall provide, for at least backfill and sub-base levels in trench reinstatements, a foamed concrete that is permeable to a degree not less than the surrounding ground. A backfill layer of pea gravel, of 100 mm minimum thickness and surrounded by a geotextile filter fabric where appropriate, may by considered to offer an equivalent drainage potential.

4)   The Authority shall notify the Undertaker, prior to excavation, of any site where high sulphate levels are known to occur. Following such notification the Undertaker shall provide a sulphate resistant foamed concrete.

A9.3   Foamed Concrete Ingredients

1)   All aggregates shall pass a 37.5 mm BS sieve and shall not contain more than 5% by weight of clay contamination, determined in accordance with BS 882: 1983 Clause 5.4.

2)   All foam concentrates shall be diluted in accordance with the manufacturer's recommendations and aerated using a appropriately designed foam generating system. Foam concentrates and diluted solutions should be stored according to the manufacturer's recommendations and used within the recommended shelf life.

3)   All accelerators, plasticisers, water reducing agents and other admixtures shall be used in accordance with the manufacturer's recommendations, subject to experience of their suitability, obtained by prior development testing.

A9.4   Foamed Concrete Production

1)   FCRs shall, normally, be prepared on site, either from basic constituents, or using a ready-mixed base mortar delivered to site. However, subject to experience, gained by prior development, that the mix is suitable for transport by road, foamed concretes may be partially or wholly mixed away from the site.

2)   FCRs shall be prepared in accordance with a mix formulation proven, by prior development testing, to yield a crushing strength within the required range. Modifications to the mix proportions, changes in aggregate type etc. or the addition of admixtures should not be undertaken without confirmation of their suitability, obtained by prior development testing.

3)   The wet density of the foamed concrete should be checked when required prior to placement. Depending on the method of foam concrete manufacture, the quality of foam manufactured on site should be checked when required prior to addition to the mix.

4)   All metering or weighing apparatus should be calibrated regularly. All mixing equipment should be maintained in accordance with the manufacturer's recommendations and checked regularly.

5)   FCRs of density lower than 1000 kg/m^3 will not necessarily displace standing water. A minimum density of 1050 kg/m^3 is recommended for use in excavations where standing water is present. FCRs may flow into, and block, any damaged drainage or ducting existing within, or immediately adjacent to, the excavation; where required, plastic sheeting etc. may provide adequate protection during pouring and curing.

6)   FCRs shall not be tamped, or otherwise compacted, unless specifically required, and then only in accordance with the manufacturer's recommendations.

7)   Reinstatement of the surface layers shall not be carried out until the foamed concrete has attained sufficient strength to allow adequate compaction of bituminous materials. A simple penetration or indentation test is recommended to allow confirmation of adequate strength prior to surfacing. Any standardised test procedure can be used and, with prior experience, will indicate the earliest time at which surfacing can be carried out. FCRs are unlikely to provide significant load bearing capacity for several hours after mixing, depending on ambient temperature. During this time, unguarded reinstatements can represent a hazard for children and animals etc.

Appendix A10

Permanent Cold-lay Surfacing Materials - (PCSMs)

A10.1 Introduction

Conventional hot-laid bitumen macadams generally require the use of heated and/or insulated transport and are especially difficult to lay where the required quantity is small and/or the site is a considerable distance from the nearest coating plant. The use of cold-lay surfacing materials, formulated to provide an installed performance equivalent to hot-laid materials but remaining workable for several days, at least, without degradation during storage and transport, may allow a higher degree of immediate permanent reinstatement for small or remote excavations that represent much of a utility's typical workload. Such materials have been termed Permanent Cold-lay Surfacing Materials (PCSMs) and will incorporate the following basic principles:

1)   Adequate performance will be achieved by the use of proprietary binder formulations, with no additional solvent diluents added subsequent to manufacture. Base binder material types and any additives are restricted only by the need to provide an adequate performance and reasonable visual match to conventional materials.

2)   Mix formulations shall be in general accordance with BS4987:1988 where relevant, and as amended by the overriding necessity to provide grading and mixing requirements appropriate to the binder formulation and to facilitate compaction to a dense condition.

3)   Mixes may incorporate crushed rock aggregates, artificial (including slag) aggregates or natural gravel aggregates, provided that each combination of aggregate type and binder, as required, is proven suitable by separate approval testing. Nominal aggregate size shall be as specified for the relevant hot-laid material option.

4)   All PCSMs shall require approval, by performance testing, in accordance with Section A10.3 or Section A10.4. The overall material formulation, manufacture and placement are limited only by the need to satisfy the remaining requirements of Appendix A10 of this specification.

A10.2 General Requirements

Approved PCSMs may be used in substitution of any bitumen macadams permitted for use by this specification, at the discretion of the Utilities, as follows:

a)   As interim materials, at any position, in all reinstatements.

b)   As permanent materials, in any position, in all footway, footpath and cycletrack reinstatements.

c)   As permanent basecourse material (PCBC) in all Type 3 and 4 roads.

d)   As permanent wearing course material (PCWC) in all Type 2, 3 and 4 roads.

All PCSMs shall be laid and compacted in accordance with Appendix A8.

A10.3 Approval Procedure - Footways, Footpaths and Cycletracks

1)   The Undertaker shall select the permanent cold-lay binder, aggregate type and a suitable reinstatement test site, and shall notify the Authority accordingly.

2)   The Undertakers, or their contractors, shall carry out the test reinstatement in accordance with Section S8.

3)   A joint inspection shall be arranged at the end of the permanent guarantee period, to assess the test reinstatement ,and to establish its compliance with the required performance criteria. In the event of any Authority failing to attend such a joint inspection, the Undertaker shall complete the assessment and provide copies of all measurements and photographs etc. to the Authority.

71

F

4)   Where the assessment confirms that the test reinstatement complies with all relevant performance criteria specified in Section S2, the combination of permanent cold-lay binder and aggregate type tested shall be deemed suitable for permanent use in footways, footpaths and cycletracks. The permanent cold-lay mix formulation shall then be approved nationally for unrestricted use, in footways, footpaths and cycletracks only, in the layer thicknesses shown in Appendix A7.

A10.4 Approval Procedure - Roads

1)   The permanent cold-lay mix formulation shall be tested in accordance with the procedure specified in Section A10.3 for footways, footpaths and cycletracks, except that the test reinstatement shall be carried out in a road and in accordance with Section S6.

2)   Following successful completion of the foregoing test procedure, the Undertaker shall extract a minimum of 6 x 100 mm diameter core samples from the test reinstatement. The Undertaker shall provide 2 working days notice for the Authority to witness the coring operation.

3)   A Repeated Load Indirect Tensile (RLIT) test shall be carried out on a minimum of six core samples and the elastic stiffness modulus determined.   The testing shall be carried out using the Nottingham Asphalt Tester (NAT) apparatus , with a pulsed vertical force equivalent to a load of 150 N per 750 mm^2 of specimen cross-sectional area, calculated to the nearest 150 N.   Each test pulse shall be applied for a period of 125 $\pm$10 milliseconds, during which the test load shall be gradually increased up to the required value.   A total of 5 conditioning pulses shall be applied, followed by 5 test pulses, all at 20°C.   The RLIT test and reporting procedure shall be in accordance with BS DD 91/13086 : 1991.

4)   A uniaxial creep (UC) test shall be carried out using the original 6 core samples, after RLIT testing, or using a minimum of 6 further samples obtained from the same coring operation, and the resistance to permanent deformation plotted.   The testing shall be carried out using the NAT apparatus, at 100 kPa axial test stress and 40°C; with a 10 minute conditioning period, 60 minute test duration and 15 minute relaxation period.   The UC test and reporting procedure shall be in accordance with BS DD 185 : 1990.

An alternative test procedure is permitted for the determination of the creep resistance of a PCSM. A wheel tracking test, similar in principle to the BS DD 184 : 1990 test, may be carried out, using appropriate slab samples cut from the test reinstatement.

5)   The results obtained from each set of core samples shall be averaged, excluding the highest and lowest result, and the average value of elastic stiffness (MPa) obtained.   The average value of elastic stiffness shall not be less than the relevant minimum requirement shown in Table A10.1 for 100 pen hot material.   The resistance to permanent deformation, determined by the NAT apparatus or a wheel tracking test, shall show an acceptable characteristic.

6)   Subject to proven compliance with Table A10.1, the combination of permanent cold-lay binder and aggregate type tested shall be deemed to be equivalent to the relevant 100 pen hot-laid macadam and to be suitable for permanent use in roads, footways, footpaths and cycletracks.   The permanent cold-lay mix formulation shall then be approved nationally for use in flexible, composite, rigid and modular roads, all as permitted and in the road categories and layer thicknesses shown in Appendices A3, A4, A5 and A6 respectively.   The mix formulation shall also be approved nationally for unrestricted use in footways, footpaths and cycletracks, in the layer thicknesses shown in Appendix A7.

7)   Where the average elastic stiffness value is not less than the relevant minimum requirement shown in Table A10.1 for 50 pen hot material, and the resistance to permanent deformation shows an acceptable characteristic, the permanent cold-lay mix formulation shall be deemed to be equivalent to the relevant 50 pen hot-laid macadam. The mix formulation shall be approved nationally as specified in Section A10.3. 6), except that the layer thicknesses may be reduced in accordance with Appendix A11.

8)   Where the average elastic stiffness value exceeds the relevant minimum requirement shown in Table A10.1 for 200 pen hot material but does not equal the relevant minimum requirements shown for 100 pen hot material, and the resistance to permanent deformation shows an acceptable characteristic, the permanent cold-lay mix formulation shall be deemed to be equivalent to the relevant 200 pen hot-laid macadam, at least.   The mix formulation shall be approved nationally as specified in Section A10.3 6), except that the layer thicknesses shall be increased in accordance with Appendix A11 for 200 pen material.

Equivalence to any intermediate pen value, say 150 pen, may be calculated by interpolation and the layer thicknesses increased to an appropriate intermediate value, determined pro rata in accordance with Appendix A11.

Permanent Cold-lay Surfacing Material	Minimum Property Requirement at 20°C for Equivalence to :		
	50 pen hot-laid Elastic stiffness (MPa)	100 pen hot-laid Elastic stiffness (MPa)	200 pen hot-laid Elastic stiffness (MPa)
20 mm nom. size Basecourse	4600	2400	900
10 mm nom. size Wearing course	3800	1900	800
6 mm nom. size Wearing course	2800	1400	600
All materials	Uniaxial creep (resistance to permanent deformation) NAT test : Results shall be plotted as microstrain vs. time (seconds as horizontal axis). The characteristic shall exhibit a distinct stabilisation during the first 2000 seconds, a near horizontal final phase and shall not exceed 10,000 microstrain at any time during the test. **Note 1** : A wheel-tracking test is permitted as an alternative to the NAT test **Note 2** : The tabulated values are provisional and may be subject to review.		

Table A10.1 - Minimum permanent cold-lay surfacing material requirements

F*

Appendix A11

Bitumen Binder Equivalence

A11.1 Roadbase and Basecourse Reinstatement

1) The layer thickness requirements of this specification, for bituminous roadbase and basecourse materials, are based on the following:

   a) A 100 pen grade bitumen binder for the manufacture of 20 mm nominal size dense bitumen basecourse macadam, used as a combined roadbase/basecourse, or as basecourse only.

   b) A 50 pen grade bitumen binder for the manufacture of 50/20 hot rolled asphalt basecourse, used as a combined roadbase/basecourse or as basecourse only.

2) Alternative binder grades may be used, as shown in Table A11.1, provided that the layer thickness is amended to that shown in the table.

Material	Bitumen Stiffness	Combined Roadbase / Basecourse (mm)				Basecourse only (mm)	
		Road Type				Road Type	
		1	2	3	4	3	4
20 mm DBC	200 pen	Not permitted	275	215	155	85	85
	100 pen	260	210	150	110	60	60
	70 pen	215	180	135	105	60	60
	50 pen	200	165	120	100	60	60
50/20 HRABC	100 pen	Not permitted	275	215	155	85	85
	70 pen	Not permitted	245	190	135	75	75
	50 pen	260	210	150	110	60	60

Table A11.1 - Roadbase and Basecourse Thickness

A11.2 Wearing Course Reinstatement

1) The layer thickness requirements of this specification, for bituminous wearing course materials, are based on the following:

   a) A 100 pen grade binder for the manufacture of 10 mm nominal size close graded or 6 mm nominal size dense bitumen wearing course macadams.

   b) A 50 pen grade binder for the manufacture of 30/14 hot rolled asphalt wearing course.

2) Alternative binder grades may be used, as shown in Table A11.2. No alteration in thickness is permitted.

Material	Bitumen Stiffness	Wearing Course in Road Type			
		1	2	3	4
6mm	200 pen	Not permitted	Not permitted	✓	✓
DBWC	100 pen	✓	✓	✓	✓
& 10mm	70 pen	✓	✓	✓	✓
CGWC	50 pen	✓	✓	✓	✓
	100 pen	Not permitted	Not permitted	✓	✓
30/14	70 pen	Not permitted	✓	✓	✓
HRAWC	50 pen	✓	✓	✓	✓

Table A11.2 - Permitted Binder - Wearing course

Note : Tables A11.1 and A11.2 do not permit the use of 200 pen, 100 pen or 70 pen binders in certain instances for road types 1 and 2; this is to limit possible premature failure during the intended structural life of the reinstatement. The surfacing materials concerned are likely to deform at an unacceptable rate.

Notes For Guidance

NG1.   Introduction

NG1.1   General

1)   The primary objective of this specification is to ensure that all Undertakers' reinstatements within highways are completed, to a permanent standard, as soon as is practicable and to a consistently high quality. Undertakers' and Authority personnel will be required to work together, in close co-operation, in order to achieve this objective. The reinstatement structure assumed to be typical, in most cases, is the flexible road structure shown in Figure NG1.1.

Figure NG1.1 - Flexible Road Structure

2)   This specification may require a joint inspection of the site to be made, depending on the existing site conditions, before the commencement of works. Such joint pre-inspections may be of an informal nature, according to mutual agreement, and should be carried out at the earliest convenience of both parties.

3)   This specification may require a formal notification of circumstances or requirements, depending on the existing site conditions, before the commencement of works. Such pre-notifications should be issued at the earliest possible opportunity. Undertakers shall comply with such notification issued at the street works notice stage, and should make reasonable efforts to comply with notification issued later.

4)   Where this specification allows several options, it is recommended, wherever practicable, to agree a preferred option from the alternatives available. This principle should be applied to all sections where alternatives are provided.

NG1.2　Guarantee Period

1)　Where an Authority intends to resurface or reconstruct a section of road the Undertaker may, by agreement, complete any reinstatement to a mutually agreed interim standard. The guarantee period will thereafter be waived, unless the Undertaker's reinstatement can be shown to be grossly substandard. It is expected that agreement to this procedure will be conditional upon the Undertaker paying to the Authority half of the savings made by not carrying out a permanent reinstatement.

2)　Where site circumstances are considered to militate against a successful permanent reinstatement, an additional interim period of up to a further 6 months may be adopted, before it is nessary to complete the permanent reinstatement.

NG1.3　Road Categories

1)　The national network of roads carrying up to 30 m.s.a. within a 20 year period, classified according to the requirements of this specification, will yield a distribution similar to that shown in Table NG1.1. It is expected that the roads in any Authority area will show a similar distribution although there will be some local variations. In future years there will be cases where traffic flows change to such a degree that reclassification will be necessary. It is expected that reclassification to a lower category will frequently occur, as well as reclassification to a higher category.

Road Type	% of Total
1	1
2	5
3	9
4	85

Table NG1.1 - Estimated highway classification

2)　For any road, its m.s.a. rating gives the number of standard axle loads which it is expected to carry over a defined period of time. In the context of the reinstatement of openings in highways, materials and thicknesses have been specified to give a satisfactory service life, based on the m.s.a. rating, over a 20 year period. The m.s.a. is calculated using the following input data :

    a) Initial 24 hour annual average daily flow of commercial vehicles in one direction (per lane where appropriate).
    b) Estimated annual growth rate of commercial vehicles over the 20 year period.
    c) Average vehicle axle factor over the 20 year service life.

This data can be processed by DEFLEC or PAVSCAN software or by the use of the TRRL PA/SCR 243 nomograph or TRRL LR1132 procedures, which allow local knowledge of traffic growth, traffic patterns and commercial vehicle type and loading to be taken into account in the categorisation of road types.

3)　Where an existing road is near or beyond its working life and is expected to be reconstructed within the foreseeable future, it is recommended that all parties meet to consider any road reclassification that may be advisable. It may also be appropriate to agree amendments to methods, materials or performance where such roads are expected to be reconstructed within the guarantee period.

NG1.5　Alternative Options

1)　New Materials
Research into new or improved reinstatement materials is known to be being undertaken by many organisations and this work may well produce materials that perform as well as or better than those specified in this specification. In order to allow these materials to be proven by development testing, the materials and layer thicknesses quoted in this specification may be altered or supplemented, subject to prior mutual agreement.

2)　Local Materials
Materials may be available locally that cannot be specified in any national specification, but which, by experience, are known to give acceptable performance in service. In order to allow the use of such proven

local materials, and subject to prior mutual agreement, the materials and layer thicknesses quoted in this specification may be amended.

3) Compaction Equipment
Alternative compaction plant, including new compaction equipment and lightweight versions of conventional compaction plant may be used, in principle, subject to the availability of an operational procedure that has been proven by development testing to be capable of achieving the same degree of compaction as any option shown in Appendix A8.

NG1.6   Immediate Works

40 mm of bituminous surfacing material is the minimum required by Section S1.6.1. A greater thickness may be required, for heavy traffic application or where roads are subjected to frequent traffic for the full 10 days permitted duration, if further remedial works are to be avoided.

NG1.7   Services within Road Structure

1)   Some apparatus exists at shallow depth within the existing road structure and special requirements may apply to reinstatement. Both the Undertaker and the Authority are likely to have particular criteria and this specification may be altered or supplemented, subject to prior mutual agreement to accommodate any such requirements.

2)   Not all new apparatus will need to be installed to the full depth or width expected by this specification, an example is cable TV. This specification may be altered or supplemented subject to prior mutual agreement.

NG2. Performance Requirements

NG2.2.2 Edge Depression - Intervention
The freedom from excessive trips for pedestrians and stability for two wheeled vehicles are considered to be the main requirements. Given that pedestrians and various two wheeled vehicles are likely to use or cross any roads, footways and cycle tracks, it is considered necessary to set a single limit for edge depressions.

NG2.2.3 Surface Depression - Intervention
Excessively deep depressions will reduce ride quality and give rise to noise and vibration. The maximum depth of surface depression within the area of a reinstatement is limited to approximately 2.5% of the width of reinstatement, which represents a mean slope of 1 in 20 (5% gradient). In order to prevent excessive areas of standing water, it is considered necessary to limit the maximum depth of a surface depression to 25 mm, regardless of the width of reinstatement.

NG2.2.4 Surface Crowning - Intervention
Excessively high crowning of a reinstatement will reduce ride quality and give rise to noise and vibration. The maximum height of crowning within the area of a reinstatement is limited to approximately 2.5% of the width of the reinstatement, which represents a mean slope of 1 in 20 (5% gradient). In order to prevent excessive surface irregularity, it is considered necessary to limit the maximum height of crowning to 25 mm, regardless of the width of reinstatement.

NG2.2.5 Combined Defect Intervention
The intervention limits specified for surface depressions and surface crowning include a reduction in the intervention limit, to 80% of the tabulated value, subject to a minimum of 10 mm, where surface depressions and/or crowning and/or edge depressions overlap. The individual features shall be measured, and the reduction applied, as follows:

1) Combination Depressions
Where an edge depression overlaps an area of surface depression, then the area of overlapping depression should be measured as shown in Figure NG2.2. Any surface crowning also overlapping the area of combined depressions should be measured separately, as shown in Figure NG2.3.

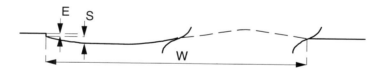

Figure NG2.2 - Combination Depression

E = edge depression contribution   = 10mm

S = surface depression contribution   = 10mm or   } whichever is
                                               = 80% tabulated value   } the greater

The depth of a combination depression is further limited, if the depression results in standing water.

2) Combination Crowning

Where an area of surface crowning overlaps an edge depression or a surface depression or any combination thereof, then the area of overlapping crowning should be measured as shown in Figure NG2.3. The area of overlapping depression should be measured separately, as shown in Figure NG2.2.

Figure NG2.3 - Combination Crowning

C = Surface depression contribution   = 10mm or   ⎫ whichever is
                                        = 80% tabulated value ⎭ the greater

The maximum height of combination crowning is further limited if the crowning results in standing water.

NG2.3 Fixed Features

Fixed features, e.g. kerbstones and related precast concrete products, channel blocks and drainage fixtures, surface boxes and ironware, should be bedded on a sound foundation, in accordance with the owner's requirements. In order to prevent excessive areas of standing water, it is considered necessary to set separate intervention limits for channel blocks, drainage fixtures, surface boxes and ironware.

NG2.4 Surface Regularity

Where the use of a rolling straightedge is not permitted, the surface regularity shall be assessed on some mutually agreed basis. One method could be the use of a 2 metre or 3 metre straightedge.

NG2.5 Structural Integrity

1)   Reinstatement materials and compaction requirements have been specified in order to safeguard the pavement structure both within and adjacent to the reinstatement. Any substantial or rapid settlement within a reinstatement may therefore indicate a potential reduction in the stability of the adjacent pavement structure, as well as potential defects in the reinstatement.

2)   There will be cases, in adverse circumstances where the correct application of this specification in all respects will still result in levels of settlement within the reinstatement that do not meet the requirements of Section S2.5, Structural Integrity. For example, the type and condition of the adjacent structure may limit the degree of compaction that can be achieved, so influencing the amount of settlement that could occur.

3)   Any engineering investigation is intended only to determine the likelihood and extent of any further settlement and the most cost-effective and convenient method of restoring the structural stability and surface performance of the failed sections of a reinstatement to a satisfactory condition. In the case of large or deep excavations, it may be appropriate to agree an extended interim guarantee period, with additional interim surfacing materials laid to restore the running surface. When no further consolidation is considered likely, a permanent basecourse and wearing course may be laid and the permanent guarantee period initiated. In any event, the location and extent of any re-excavation should be mutually agreed, taking full advantage of any bound materials already laid.

4)   The depth of unbound materials is the difference in vertical height between the underside of the lowest bound material and the trench bed, or the top of the surround material if that itself is bound.

NG2.6 Skid Resistance

1)   An adequate skid resistance of the reinstated running surface must be maintained by control of the texture depth and the polished stone value (PSV) of the aggregate exposed at the road surface; being pre-coated chippings rolled into the surface (HRA) or coarse aggregate at the wearing course surface (coated macadams) or any chippings or fine aggregate applied in any form of surface dressing or slurry sealing treatment.

2)   In order to minimise the need to carry out skid resistance measurements on existing running surfaces, it is recommended that Authorities provide relevant information wherever available.

3)   Smaller reinstatements constitute a much lower degree of skidding risk.   However, material requirements and laying conditions remain unchanged and it is expected that the skid resistance properties of smaller reinstatements will not be significantly different. Measurements of skid resistance, riding quality and surface texture become progressively more difficult as the reinstatement width reduces. The TRRL Mini Texture Meter is some 600 mm wide and should never be used on trenches of a lesser width. The actual minimum practicable width will depend on the trench realignment and radius of curvature. Similarly, the sand patch method becomes increasingly inaccurate or imprecise as the volume of sand is reduced, Table S2.6 gives the absolute minimum for the current BS 598 sand patch method. Care must be taken to ensure that the resultant circle is wholly within the reinstatement area. Section S2.6.2 gives the facility, subject to prior mutual agreement, for using a modified sand patch method but the use of any lesser quantity of sand will result in greater imprecision. As with the texture meter and sand patch test, the TRRL Rolling Straightedge and TRRL Portable Skid-Resistance Tester should always be contained within the limits of the trench reinstatement. This can be particularly difficult with the rolling straightedge, especially when testing on a radius close to the minimum permitted by the specification. Similar criteria to the Mini Texture Meter and sand patch method apply to the use of the portable skid tester and careful siting is necessary to ensure that results are representative of the surface being tested. Given good site conditions, it is possible to obtain reasonably representative measurements of surface regularity, skid resistance and surface texture on narrower reinstatements but amended test procedures and/or extra care are required.

NG3. Excavation

1)   Where possible, all excavations should be planned before commencement of works on site. Where required, there must be sufficient quantities of appropriate materials available to provide safe trench support.

2)   Work must be undertaken and supervised by properly qualified personnel.

3)   Care must be taken when cutting surface layers in order to avoid undue damage to the running surface or to the bond between wearing course and basecourse material. Cutting by machine, e.g. road saw, chain excavator or planer, is preferred.

4)   Particular attention is drawn to the need to excavate carefully where trees, shrubs and other planted areas are involved.

NG4. Surround to Apparatus

1)   It is often necessary for an Undertaker to require special protective components and/or a specific type or quality of material to be laid within the immediate vicinity of certain types of underground apparatus. Such material is usually referred to as the surround to the apparatus, and may include tiles, covers, tubular shields, bound materials or fine unbound granular materials or any combination thereof. The resulting surround may be required for a variety of reasons including structural support, low corrosion potential, protective surround for non-metallic materials or coatings, etc. The nature of the apparatus and/or the protective features of the surround may also impose restrictions on the type of compaction equipment and procedures that can be used on any fine unbound granular materials (usually referred to as finefill) that may be used.   However, the entire surrounding effectively forms the foundation element of the reinstatement and must offer adequate support for the remainder of the reinstatement, and be capable of transmitting the imposed loading to the subgrade below the apparatus.

2)   In selecting a surround, the Undertaker should bear in mind the potential for the migration of fines from the adjacent ground (and the backfill) into open-textured surround. Such action normally results in settlement of the adjacent ground (and/or the backfill). Migration of fines can be prevented by using a close textured surround or, if this is undesirable, by enclosing the surround within a suitable filter membrane.

NG5. Backfill

NG5.1 Backfill Material Classification

For guidance, the assumed limiting performances of the five classes of backfill materials are :

Class A	Over 15% CBR
Class B	7% to 15% CBR
Class C	4% to 7% CBR
Class D	2% to 4% CBR
Class E	Less than 2% CBR (Unacceptable)

Certain materials and mixtures may be treated with cement or other agents and rendered suitable for use at backfill and/or sub-base levels provided that either the stabilisation process and laying/compaction procedures have been agreed in advance with the Authority, or the engineering properties of the stabilised material have been assessed and structural equivalence with other options is maintained.

NG5.4 Additional Requirements

Frost Heave Susceptibility

a)   The frost heave test described in BS 812 part 124 is costly and time consuming and is not suitable for routine on site control checks. The test is primarily intended as a method to establish whether or not an aggregate from a particular source is likely to be frost susceptible when used in road pavement construction. Material for the frost heave test must be representative of the source or sub-grade encountered. Authorities usually maintain a list of "Approved suppliers of non-frost susceptible materials" and should have a knowledge of frost susceptible type sub-grades in their locality. The following notes on identification of potentially frost heave susceptible material are for guidance but are not in themselves exhaustive.

b)   Clay materials can be regarded as non-frost susceptible, particularly when the plasticity index is greater than 15%. Clay/silt mixtures are more difficult to assess and will probably come in the marginal category. Silts, particularly those with a high percentage of material passing 75 micron BS test sieve (greater than10%), are likely to be frost susceptible. For cohesive/granular materials the silt fraction and particularly the quantity and type of granular aggregate will be a controlling feature. A large proportion of these mixtures are frost susceptible. If the aggregate is itself of a frost susceptible type then it is very probable that the mixture will also be frost susceptible.

c)   Granular materials with greater than 10% passing 75 micron BS sieve size have a high potential for frost susceptibility and are likely to be frost susceptible for percentages greater than 12%. All crushed chalks are frost susceptible and the magnitude of the frost heave increases with the saturation moisture content of the chalk. Similarly oolitic and magnesium limestones are likely to be frost susceptible, particularly those where the aggregate saturation moisture content exceeds 3.5%. Hard carboniferous limestones are unlikely to be frost susceptible unless they have been contaminated with clay or have a percentage passing 75 micron in excess of 12%. Similarly, crushed granites will only be frost susceptible if the percentage passing 75 micron exceeds 12% and is partially plastic. 'As dug' sands and gravels are frequently frost susceptible especially if the percentage passing 75 micron BS sieve size is greater than 12% or if it is plastic. Sands and gravels won by "wet working" techniques are unlikely to be frost susceptible unless contaminated by a clay or a high silt fraction. Man-made aggregate such as burnt colliery shales, slags and pulverised fuel ashes are peculiar materials, and it is not possible to give a note for guidance to the potential for frost heave resistance. Each source is different and will need to be assessed by the frost heave test. The exception to this rule is graded bottom furnace ash produced by modern power stations which has been found to be non-frost susceptible.

d)   Foamed concretes can generally be regarded as non-frost susceptible.

NG6. Flexible and Composite Roads

NG6.2 Sub-Base Reinstatement

1) It is expected that a bituminous sub-base will only be selected where the road-base is also bituminous.

2) When placing bituminous material directly on to the backfill it is important to ensure that the exposed surface of the backfill has been compacted. This operation is essential to minimise the risk of a build up of pore water pressure causing the subgrade to become spongy. It is also imperative that construction is phased such that any excavated areas are covered the same day with the first layer of bituminous material to prevent the ingress of water. Care should be taken in the compaction of this first layer. If pore water pressure builds up in the backfill at this stage then rolling should cease and the material left overnight or longer if necessary, prior to the placement of any further layers.

NG6.5 Edge Requirements

1) Edge regularity requirements are intended to provide a shape that will not hinder the proper compaction of material adjacent to the excavation edge. The final shape, when viewed from above, should be governed by the following general principles rather than by aesthetic considerations:

   i) There is no requirement to trim the sides of trench excavations solely to provide a uniform width, provided that individual projections are not less than 250mm in length, measured parallel to the nominal centreline of the trench.

   ii) There is no requirement to trim a small excavation solely in order to provide a square or rectangular shape. Any shape with included angles not less than 90° and with no projection less than 250mm length, may be considered to be regular.

   iii) Where sound surfacing material exists at the corner of an excavation there is no necessity to cut out to a corner; a regular chamfer may be preferable.

   iv) Where a 90° corner is to be cut out, overlapping cross cuts should be minimal and all cuts extending into the existing surface should be filled with sealant.

2) Edge sealant materials are generally based on rapid curing anionic or cationic bitumen emulsions to BS 434, typically 50 or 70 pen and approximately 70% bitumen content, or hot bitumens to BS 3690, 50 or 70 pen. An increasing range of high build and rubberised edge sealants are becoming available and, in general, are preferred. The use of high build liquid sealants or solid sealing strips etc., on a trial basis at least, is recommended.

3) Tack coating materials are generally based on rapid curing anionic or cationic bitumen emulsions to BS 434, with approximately 40% bitumen content. New tack coating materials are becoming available, and the trial use of more modern variants is recommended.

NG6.6 Special Materials

1) Special friction coatings are likely to be either calcined bauxite epoxy resin systems, special textured slurry seals or premium surface dressing applications. They will usually have been laid for safety reasons and their early reinstatement will be important.

2) The use of warning signs, e.g. "temporary road surface", should be considered until such time as the special surface can be restored.

NG7. Rigid and Modular Roads

NG7.1 Reinstatement Method

The requirements of this specification are applicable to all concrete roads up to 30 msa traffic volume. However, modern concrete roads constructed in accordance with current Government standards and specifications may well incorporate special design philosophies beyond the scope of this specification. Such roads must be identified by the Authority prior to the commencement of works, so that reinstatement requirements can be agreed.

NG7.7 Modular Roads

1) When excavating in modular roads, the existing modules shall be lifted carefully and stored for re-use. Advice regarding the lifting and storing of modules is available from The Concrete Block Paving Association, Information Sheet 7 "Concrete Block Paving - Reinstatement After Trench Opening", published by Interpave.

2) It is particularly important to ensure that bedding and jointing sands should meet the performance demands in areas subject to heavy vehicular traffic.

NG8. Footways, Footpaths and Cycletracks

NG8.3 Surface Reinstatement

1) High Duty and High Amenity

In high duty footways the durability of the wearing surface is of prime importance and simple cosmetic matching of materials may not be adequate. Specific grades of material such as York stone modules, or specific types of construction such as asphalt sandcarpet/mastic, may have been laid in order to give an acceptable performance under extreme conditions and similar materials will need to be reinstated. In high amenity footways the cosmetic matching of materials at the wearing surface may be of primary importance with durability of secondary importance.

2) Other Macadam

A wide range of surface treatments exist, commonly of much less than 6 mm aggregate size. Where available, a similar surface finish will be reinstated. The wearing course material may be reinstated using any of the allowed basecourse or wearing course materials, with a final surface treatment applied as soon as practicable following the laying of the permanent wearing course.

3) Modular Footways

All Authorities are recommended to retain stocks of modules used within their area to enable them to provide replacements when required. Where replacements are required due to breakages caused during Undertakers' works, the Authority must provide replacements, where stocks are available, to the relevant Undertaker at reasonable cost. Where replacements are required due to breakage at some time prior to the Undertakers' works, the Authority must provide replacements to the Undertaker free of charge.

NG8.7 Excavations Adjacent to Roads

The most heavily stressed area of a road is usually the inside wheel track adjacent to the road edge. Depending on ground conditions, it is often necessary to support the road edge by providing lateral restraint within the adjoining footway, footpath, cycletrack or verge. The most common form of edge support is a section of unbound or cement bound granular materials. This construction will most commonly be encountered when the horizontal distance between the edge of the Undertakers' excavation and the edge of the road surface is less than the expected depth of cover of the Undertakers' apparatus.

NG9. Verges

No 'Notes for Guidance' for this Section.

NG10. Compaction

NG10.1/NG10.2 Cohesive and Granular Materials

For cohesive or granular materials a vibrating roller will often be unsuitable in small excavations due to the restricted manoeuvrability of large heavy rollers required to give adequate levels of compaction within an acceptable number of passes.

NG10.3 Bituminous Materials

Certain combinations of compaction plant and bituminous materials are likely to result in surface cracking, the development of shear surfaces and/or crushing of aggregate as the material approaches maximum density, if compaction is continued. Provided that the material has been laid and compacted within the appropriate ternperature range, fewer passes will be allowed if any of the above circumstances become apparent.

NG10.5 Modular Surfacing Materials

Depending on the size and type of paving module to be laid, and/or the extent of the area to be surfaced etc., the use of additional mechanical compaction may become necessary.

NG10.6 Equipment Operation and Restrictions

NG10.6.1 Compaction Procedure
1)   A single pass of any compaction plant is deemed to be completed when the entire surface area of the layer has been impacted by the foot, roll or plate of the compaction device. Where the excavation width is more than 50 mm greater than the foot, roll or plate width (i.e. the side clearance between the compacting surface and the wall of the excavation exceeds 25 mm per side) two or more traverses of the compaction device will be required to ensure coverage of the entire surface and all will be deemed to constitute a single compactive pass. Compaction plant should be steered along a line offset from that steered on the previous pass so that alternate passes are run close in to each side wall of the excavation.

2)   Small items of compaction plant will frequently be required and additional provisions need to be considered for use in trenches of less than 200mm width, small excavations and other areas of restricted access.   In general, lightweight vibrotampers and hydraulic or pneumatic poletampers are capable of achieving the same degree of compaction as the heavier items of plant specified in Appendix A8. However, such small plant is invariably not self-advancing and therefore more difficult to specify. Currently there is no alternative equipment available for this application and the provisions included in Appendix A8 are proven in practice.

NG10.6.2 Equipment Maintenance
All vibrating compaction plant must be checked regularly and adjusted as required in order to ensure that the manufacturer's recommended operating frequency is maintained throughout the working life of the plant.

NG10.6.3 Hand Rammers
Hand rammers may be used for initial tamping of fine fill material or immediately adjacent to street furniture, reinstatement edges etc. In all cases full machine compaction complying with Appendix A8 will normally be applied immediately after the required thickness of material has been built-up. However, hand ramming alone may be necessary around stand pipes and other isolated obstructions.

NG10.6.4 Percussive Rammers
A percussive rammer is an electric, pneumatic or hydraulically operated impactor adapted for compaction purposes by the fitting of a flat faced compaction foot. The foot shall not exceed 200 mm width or contact length.

NG10.6.5 Vibrating Plates
Vibrating plate compactors should be operated in the lowest available gear, except for the first pass which should be at maximum forward speed.

NG10.6.6 Vibrotampers

1)   Vibrotampers are likely to be the most commonly used means of compaction for Undertakers' reinstatements, and may be operated at reduced speed, for the first pass only, with cohesive materials. The use of vibrotampers is not permitted in certain circumstances with cohesive or bituminous materials, as detailed in Appendix A8. Vibrotampers are permitted under all other circumstances but are not preferred for any permanent wearing course application or any other application involving layer thicknesses of less than 50 mm.

2)   Vibrotampers 25 to 50 kg - The foot shall not exceed 150 mm width and 200 mm contact length.

3)   Vibrotampers over 50 kg - The width of the foot must not exceed 5 mm per kg of the nominal operational mass of the vibrotamper. The contact length of the foot must not be less than 175 mm or greater than 350 mm; the contact area of the foot must not exceed 1000 mm^2 per kg of the nominal mass. The mass of any extension leg shall not exceed 10% of the nominal operational mass of the vibrotamper.

NG10.6.7   Vibrating Rollers

1)   Vibrating rollers are the preferred method of compaction for all permanent wearing courses. A twin drum vibrating roller shall include two vibrating rolls. A twin drum roller in which one roll vibrates shall be deemed to be a single drum vibrating roller. The mass per metre width of the roller is calculated by dividing the total effective mass supported by the roll or rolls by the total effective width of the roll or rolls.

2)   Vibrating rollers should be operated in the lowest available gear. The first pass of any vibrating roller should be carried out without vibration in order to nip in the material adjacent to the reinstatement edges and to prevent uneven displacement of material within the remainder of the reinstatement area. All remaining passes specified must be carried out with full vibration.

3)   A minimum mass of 600 kg per metre width is required for vibrating rollers for the compaction of bituminous material. However, many bituminous footways and footpaths throughout the UK have been constructed to a standard that is significantly inferior to any current standard. Clearly any damage caused to the surrounding footway or footpath by the use of this plant would be unfortunate and Undertakers shall not be liable for the repair of any such damage. Where an existing structure, road, footway, footpath or cycletrack may be marked or otherwise damaged by the use of a 600-1000 kg per metre width vibrating roller, it will be the responsibility of the Authority to notify the Undertaker accordingly whereupon the use of a lower weight vibrating roller will be agreed. Any damage resulting from the use of vibrating rollers of greater than 1000 kg per metre width will then be the responsibility of the Undertaker.

4)   The use of twin drum rollers is preferred to single drum for the compaction of bituminous materials. This practice will undoubtedly improve the quality of the permanent wearing course. However, single drum vibrating rollers are permitted for the compaction of bituminous materials provided that the number of passes is twice that specified for a twin drum roller of equivalent weight and provided that no more than 12 passes will be required, as detailed in Appendix A8.

NG10.6.8 Machine-mounted Compactors

All machine-mounted compaction equipment, whether integral to the vehicle design or special attachments for front or rear mounting on to the chassis or booms of any excavator, tractor or skid-steer vehicle etc. is expected to be operated in accordance with the recommendations of the compactor or attachment manufacturer, to the relevant compaction procedure required by Appendix A 8. However, other operational variables should also be considered prior to the operation of such plant as follows :

1)   Compactor Downforce

The total downforce will vary depending upon the weight of the vehicle chassis or compactor frame, and the degree of additional downforce applied by a hydraulic boom etc. However, changes in the configuration of any vehicle, by the addition or removal of other accessories etc, changes in the width of the vibrating foot, roll or plate etc, movement of any boom resulting in a significant change of loading geometry or outreach etc, attaching to other vehicles of differing types or weights etc, can all result in a reduction of compactive performance that is seldom apparent. All operators should be aware of the potential reduction in performance resulting from such changes in machine, configuration or operating procedure.

2) Applied Downforce

It is recommended that all back-hoe mounted compactors be fitted with a downforce limiting device, correctly set, or with a simple indicating device allowing the amplitude to be estimated. The mounting of compaction equipment to the front loader arms of an excavator, where the downforce is sensibly limited by the lifting of the front wheels, is preferred.

3) Compactor Set-up

Where the frequency or amplitude of vibration, or any other parameter affecting the dynamic output of a compactor is expected to be adjusted on a routine basis, all parameters should be set in accordance with the manufacturer's recommendations unless specific testing has shown other settings to be at least as effective.

NG11. Ancillary Activities

NG 11.2 Street Furniture, Special Features, Etc.

In the interests of safety generally, and particularly in the interests of the disabled, street furniture and tactile paving removed during the course of works should be replaced immediately following the completion of works. Similarly, traffic signs and road markings removed during the course of works should also be replaced immediately following completion.

NG 11.3 Traffic Sensors

1) In London the relevant Authority will be the Traffic Control Systems Unit.

2) Examples of sensors include buried traffic sensors, ice warning sensors, stainless steel road studs, thermoplastic node markers, verge mounted markers (e.g. bar strips).